Mysterious Ways

The Reverend Thornton Dixon Adams:
A Life Enriched by Giving

Timothy Roach

Archway Publishing books may be ordered through booksellers or by contacting:

Archway Publishing
1663 Liberty Drive
Bloomington, IN 47403
www.archwaypublishing.com
844-669-3957

ISBN: 978-1-6657-1143-2 (sc)
ISBN: 978-1-6657-1145-6 (hc)
ISBN: 978-1-6657-1144-9 (e)

Library of Congress Control Number: 2021917691

Print information available on the last page.

Archway Publishing rev. date: 09/10/2021

To my loving parents.
And to my dear siblings …
Susan, Jane, Michael, Sally and Dickie

Contents

An Introduction to
The Reverend Thornton Dixon Adams

My name is Dr. Gary C. Royals, and I am currently the senior pastor of the First United Methodist Church in Conover, NC. Before I assumed this role, I was the District Superintendent (DS) of the Charlotte/Metro district with over 130 churches under my supervision. It didn't take me long to "size up" the churches and pastors and to learn their strengths and weaknesses. I wouldn't take anything for what I learned during the four years I served in that capacity, as I dealt with the "good, bad and ugly."

With this fresh in my mind, I left that role and, once again, re-entered the church as pastor in 2015. When I first came to FUMC Conover, I was told that I had a retired United Methodist pastor in my congregation. With all that I had learned about pastors as a DS, my first reaction was … "oh no, not a retired Methodist pastor in my church. He will be a thorn in my side." Soon thereafter, one morning, as I was in my office, I heard a soft, gentle voice say to my administrative assistant … "is the preacher in the house?" Dixon Adams came into my office, sat down, and for the next 45 minutes we talked like we had known each other for years. I literally fell in love with this quiet, unassuming yet astute man who had given his life to God's calling.

This began a special relationship which has lasted to this day. During our times together, he has literally mesmerized me with his stories and experiences, many of which I almost found it hard to believe. He lives to bless others in simple ways ... from presenting a freshly baked loaf of bread to calling on my birthday and whistling "happy birthday." I felt myself wanting to emulate how he loved people and treated them as he desired to be treated. My fears of a "retired minister in my church" quickly dissolved as I realized how blessed I am to have such a treasure in my life. No matter how busy I am, when I hear those soft words ... "is the preacher in the house?" ... I stop what I am doing and spend time with him.

My life is richer and fuller because I have known a man whose life, actions and attitude reflect the love and grace of God. Only heaven will reveal the lives which have been impacted by the life and ministry of Dixon Adams. Through his life, we clearly see that......*God works in a mysterious way.*

Dr. Gary C. Royals

Preface

Susan is a long-time friend from Boston. Her family has a long family relationship with that of Reverend Thornton Dixon Adams.

Susan's aunt Frances, a Lieutenant Commander in the Navy and widely respected nurse in the Boston area, was married to Shockley D. Adams – "Sam" - a Navy veteran from Carthage, North Carolina.

The families shared a colorful friendship for many years. During that span, Susan came to know well and admire her uncle Sam's brother, Dixon.

Susan has long professed her admiration for the World War Two generation that endured the Depression in the 1930's and fought tyranny in the 1940's. They've often been called America's "Greatest Generation." They accomplished much, did so responsibly and with dignity, and left a noble example to those that followed. For Susan and for thousands of his friends, colleagues and fellow congregants over the years, Dixon Adams has been an exemplar of that generation.

His life has been one of quiet service, a hallmark of the Adams family for centuries in the Piedmont. He has served his country and his North Carolina community in times of joy and in moments of private heartbreak.

Two years ago, after a brief period during which Susan

had lost her aunt Frances, and shortly thereafter, her own dear mother Claire, she recounted what a source of comfort Dixon had been to her in the wake of those painful losses. She asked me to write his story.

Written over the course of a year of interviews, I came to know an exceptional man. This little book is the tale of a lifetime of giving, and a grateful testimony to a wonderful friend.

Timothy Roach

Acknowledgements

This book was begun at the suggestion of my close friend Susan, with whom Dixon has shared family, friendship, and thoughtful solace for many years. Throughout the project, Susan provided encouragement and useful professional advice. From the outset, she gave ample assistance, anecdotes about family ties, even stepping in to format the finished manuscript.

Dixon's middle son, Rodger Adams, provided invaluable technical assistance in selecting and editing photographs, adding the sensitive touch of a loving and admiring son.

Dr. Gary C. Royals wrote an appreciation of Dixon that highlighted a collegial relationship and friendship that continues to this day. He noted the irreplaceable value of humanity and kindness in someone he deems "a treasure in my life."

And most of all, Dixon Adams himself, who generously gave up nearly up a year of his Monday mornings to relate his many family recollections and moving stories of a life well-lived.

Dixon is the beating heart of this book.

*"A friend may well be considered
the masterpiece of nature."*

———

Ralph Waldo Emerson

1

A CARTHAGE FAMILY

If you were painting an idyllic portrait of small-town America, you might just choose Carthage, North Carolina.

The town is situated in the Sandhills region of the southeastern Piedmont, with a landscape of gently rolling hills, meandering streams, dense green forest, and colors that dazzle under soft blue skies in the autumn sunlight.

Agriculture was historically the backbone of the area's economy, with tobacco being the dominant crop. After the Civil War, the area expanded its economy with the building of short-line railroads. Light industry soon entered the region, establishing hundreds of factories in what became the furniture capital of the world, a major producer of textiles and a leader in the booming nineteenth century buggy industry.

North Carolina's extraordinary natural beauty made it a haven for tourists lured by its gentle climate. Just after the turn of the century, the development of golf resorts drew affluent visitors from the North and South alike. Often, after church on Sundays, our family would make the seven-mile trip to Pinehurst or Southern Pines, where we'd picnic on the lush grass and watch the golfers from a distance.

There were natural springs around Carthage. From those springs was created a man-made lake, which served as the town's main water supply. Sometime after World War Two, the town suffered a major drought, and water had to be shipped in on tanker trucks from Fort Bragg. About seven miles away was a stream called Little Creek, and a bit further away was a bigger creek called Little River. Little tributaries ran through the area and provided ample recreational opportunities for adventurous children.

The town had just 1,200 residents when I was growing up. As such, it remained a close-knit community where everybody seemed to know their neighbors and fellow townspeople well. People went to school together, played together, worshiped at the same churches, looked after each other's children, and married into each other's families. Carthage was a town where strong, lifelong bonds were formed. It was here, in this place of abiding faith and friendship that my family lived and worked and prayed for generations. And it was here, on October 8, 1926, that I was born.

My Mother named me Thornton Dixon Adams, after my Grandfather.

For many years, it remained a mystery where the name Thornton came from. I asked my Dad and he had no idea. Apparently, Mother found the name in our past and was attracted to it.

The family was descended from that of General George Washington. A more thorough search into the family's genealogy in later years revealed a Thornton family as part of that relationship. Perhaps, that solved the riddle of my first name.

Early on, Mother just called me Dicky. I've been Dixon ever since.

In 1914, little more than a decade or so before my birth, World War One began.

It had been called, much too optimistically, "the War to end all wars." The conflict eventually tore Europe apart and resulted in forty million dead and injured from 1914 through 1918. In North Carolina, the War was a calamity for individuals and families. Then, in 1918, as the War was nearing an end, the world faced a massive epidemic of Spanish flu. The flu outbreak took tens of millions more lives around the world, including more than thirteen thousand in North Carolina alone.

By 1919, the nation had emerged from those two major upheavals and started getting back to work. Optimism was renewed and the economy soon shifted into overdrive. The soldiers returned from Europe and the economy jumped back into action.

The Roaring Twenties were off and running.

Innovation was in full swing during the new decade, as consumer goods, household conveniences and new fashions for women proved irresistible to consumers.

Work-saving modern conveniences made life less tedious. Innovations in electricity, transportation, and new infant technologies created huge demand. Consumers craved washing machines, vacuum cleaners, telephones and above all, the noisy, newfangled automobiles. Banks and mortgage lenders thrived as people used easy credit to finance their dream purchases. For a while, it seemed that we were living in the very best of times.

My Dad was a banker. After graduating from high school, he'd gone to Kings Business College in Raleigh, and after college, started directly to work at Wachovia Bank in Winston-Salem.

From Wachovia, he moved on to Page Trust Company, a bank owned and run by the Page family of Aberdeen. Their business focused predominantly on the main towns in Moore County: Carthage - which was the Moore County seat - Pinehurst, Southern Pines and Aberdeen.

The 1920's brought a resurgence of spending, caused by long-delayed, pent-up demand. While working with Page Trust in Aberdeen, Dad happened to meet a local schoolteacher, Gladys West, who worked in the Aberdeen school district. In time, they started seeing a lot of one another, became engaged and then married in November 1920. A family quickly followed, with Shockley born in 1923, me in 1926, and little Hazelanne in 1929.

Dad was living with his growing family in a second-floor apartment. I still have early memories of him carrying me up and down those stairs. Our apartment was just seven doors down the way from my Granddad's house on McReynolds Street. The street was originally called Elm Street, after its rows of majestic, leafy shade trees, but as time went on, the Elms gave way to the building of sidewalks and the ever-present and destructive Dutch Elm disease.

It was a good time for the banking sector. Easy credit was the order of the day. Store owners were willing to extend credit to buyers, and the prevailing attitude through much of the country was … "Buy now, Pay later!"

Business was brisk, and Dad did well. The nation was thrilled by the newfound freedom that the War's end had given to shoppers and to investors as well. On Wall Street, stock prices soared. To the nation, it seemed like the good times would last forever.

Our family never indulged in the spending spree that captivated so many other families. We lived modestly, well within our means, and generally had everything that we needed. Most importantly, our home was filled with love and good feeling.

Mother was extremely kind and attentive to all her children. She maintained exacting standards, for the household and for the children. We felt the warmth of a woman who gave us everything she had to give.

The only shadow over the home was Mother's health.

She had been sickly for many years and her health was a constant concern. She had what was, at that time, often called "a leaking heart." There were very few days when she was able to be up and about, and eventually she was permanently sidelined. Shortly after I was born, she was diagnosed with Bright's Disease, a chronic ailment of the kidneys. Her illness kept her bedridden much of the time. I only recall one occasion on which I saw her step out of the house, when she drove Dad's old Model A Ford to pick him up after watching a baseball game.

Mother continued to rule the household with the help of a series of maids, but her mobility was steadily reduced. Her condition worsened over time, with added complications of debilitating heart disease. But she was unfailing in her love and devotion, and established a happy family home, in which we never went without the necessities. We were, in fact, among the more fortunate in our community.

We had a series of maids who lived with us to help Mother with household matters. A wonderful woman named Louise Jernigan lived with us; we were as close to her as we were to our family.

My Grandmother died in 1929, when I was just three years old. That was my earliest memory as a child and a bittersweet one. It was my first experience with personal loss.

I attended the funeral with the rest of the family and recall that everyone was dressed in black. I remember the somber faces around me.

At one point, Dad gathered me protectively in his arms as we approached the coffin. He reached down and pulled away a black veil. I looked down and saw Grandmother lying there. I certainly didn't fully comprehend all that was happening, but I saw the sadness around me and felt the comfort that our large family extended to one another.

When I was four years old, I started my early schooling. My Dad's aunt ran a kindergarten class. We lived just a few doors from her home, so it was a very short walk to school. There were just four of us in the class. Three girls and me. We listened closely to those simple early lessons. But there was also time set aside for fun.

We went to each other's birthday parties, which we always enjoyed very much. We sang songs and had Birthday cake and ice cream. We played games, too. A favorite was "Pin-the-Tail-on-the-Donkey."

And we loved to dance. My aunt would place a lighted candle in a candle holder on the floor. We'd all recite, "Jack be nimble! Jack be quick! Jack jump over the candle stick!" from the ancient nursery rhyme.

Across the street was the Methodist church. On Sundays, we'd arrive at church a bit early, and, on nice warm summer days, we'd play in the churchyard, as the congregation waited for the bell to signal the start of services. My Uncle Raymond was the church sexton; he rang the bell and pulled the rope to admit the congregants. Later, as we got a little bit older, he let my siblings and I ring the bell and pull the rope in the vestibule to let the people in. I got to know every nook and cranny of that church as a boy.

I started first grade at five. If you were six years-old before October 15, you could start first grade. Since I was just five when I started school, I remained the youngest in my class at every stage of my education. I walked to grammar school, which was located just seven or eight doors from my house. Many children were brought by their parents. But my Dad was off to work early, and Mother was sick in bed. So, at five years old, I walked to my first day of school by myself. Shockley was very protective of my little sister and me. He sometimes walked us to school and made it very clear that no one should even think about giving us a rough time. As a result, we both felt very secure with him.

When I was in first grade, Mother was convinced that my brother Shockley and I should study the violin. At her insistence, we took lessons for a while. Mr. Ponish was our teacher. He was kind and extremely patient. Shockley was three years older, so he was given a full-sized violin, while I had a child's half-sized violin.

We took lessons for a year. I tried my level best, but despite my plucky efforts, it was painfully obvious - to me, to my brother, to my Mother, and to the sainted Mr. Ponish - that, with our limited aptitude for the violin, neither of us was destined for musical triumph.

However, I did play one solo performance. I was chosen to perform at a "Tom Thumb" wedding, in which children - my friends and I - were dressed up as wedding participants.

I was dressed somewhat formally, as befit my role in the wedding. My Mother made me a new formal black suit for the occasion. My big violin solo was to be a rendition of "Twinkle, Twinkle, Little Star." I was nervous, but bravely carried on.

Mother was very proud of the handsome suit she'd made, and I was happy with the way I looked. Not surprisingly, that performance marked the beginning - and the end - of my musical career.

The little girls were dressed in their pretty party dresses, and the boys in their newly pressed suits. The mothers and fathers were beaming with pride. It was a sweet, careless day of innocent fun for parents and children alike.

As I was scratching out that little tune on my violin, few of the guests at the "wedding" that afternoon could imagine that the nation's decade-long spree was about to end.

2

HARD TIMES AND HEARTBREAK

America's Wild Party ended in 1929.

On October 29, 1929, just three weeks after my third Birthday party, Wall Street experienced its sharpest decline on record. The Crash stunned investors and brought home the fact to all Americans that we were headed for hard times ahead.

Borrowers began to default on every manner of loan, including mortgages, business loans, revolving credit at clothing and hardware stores, and broker loans taken out by investors to buy stocks on margin. As the panic spread through Wall Street, concerns quickly turned to Main Streets in small towns throughout the country.

There were even defaults of credit extended by local mom-and-pop grocery stores. I would learn many years later - after I returned from the War - that there was still a $700 balance on our family's bill at the local grocery in Carthage.

After a free-spending decade, when consumer goods could be easily bought on credit, the good times ended with an earth-shaking thud. Spending slowed dramatically, and businesses large and small began to lay off workers.

Not surprisingly, banks were among the first victims of the collapse. As borrowers defaulted on loans, the banking sector - so vibrant just a few years earlier - was decimated by loan defaults, declining demand for credit, and demands on savings deposits cash that evaporated capital.

As confidence in the banking system weakened, individual banks were faced with "bank runs." Customers lined up demanding their deposits back.

Small banks in agricultural areas were hardest hit. In North Carolina alone, three-hundred and fifty-one banks were suspended during the Depression years. The biggest casualties were small-town banks with fewer depositors.

Banks made heroic efforts to hold off the runs. At Wachovia Bank, one of the banks where Dad had worked, there were stories of bank officials openly displaying suitcases containing large stacks of cash.

The mounds of cash were prominently arrayed behind bank tellers. The idea was to persuade customers that the bank had more than enough resources to cover deposits, with the hope of discouraging withdrawals.

But, despite the bankers' encouragement, it was a very hard sell. The lines of withdrawers kept growing longer.

In short order, the Depression landed squarely on our own doorstep. I was just a little tyke when all the economic chaos was occurring, and so was generally oblivious to the severe pressures that adults were feeling. But I heard bits of worried conversation here and there among the adults and saw the concern etched in their faces.

Dad was working at Page Trust Company but saw the

increasing turmoil in the banking business and the job losses there and elsewhere.

Suddenly, he found himself out of a job and faced the same challenge as millions of other displaced workers: how to earn a living for a growing young family.

As the business slump tightened its stranglehold, available jobs were more and more scarce. Dad realized that the near-term prospects in banking were not at all promising but kept searching and digging for work wherever he could. I heard adults talk about "hard times" and discuss the need to make sacrifices.

Dad had many friends in the area and had fostered a sterling reputation over the years in all his business dealings.

Then, one day in 1929, we learned, yet again, that determination - and a generous dollop of luck - play a remarkable role in one's life.

Dad enjoyed a happy turn of fortune when he was able to land a position as a rural mail carrier. The post was a bit of a plum: it ensured a regular income even in the ravaged economy.

Initially, he had a route locally around Carthage. A year or so later, a carrier in Cameron died, and Dad was transferred to the Cameron route, seven miles from Carthage.

Times were lean, but the family had enough. We lived frugally and managed to get by better than many of our neighbors.

We ate simply, but regularly. At breakfast, we'd have oatmeal and "fat-back." That was our version of bacon for breakfast. It was cut from the side meat of the hog.

As the name implied, it was not very plentiful with meat. But you could get a slab of fat-back for a cent-and-a-half a pound. We'd buy ten pounds for fifteen cents, so it was certainly affordable. Mother would cut off a slice, roll it in flour and fry it. It was a tasty and filling breakfast for the family in the morning.

For lunch we'd have pinto beans or white beans, cornbread, maybe some turnip greens. For our evening meal, we'd have grits, gravy, and cornbread, maybe with some biscuits leftover from lunch.

Our cook Vada, who lived with us, always kept a jar of blackstrap molasses on the table. I'd spread the molasses on biscuits for a special treat.

My parents used their ingenuity to make up for their limited cash resources. At one point, Dad bought the family a cow, which ensured that the children always had a daily supply of fresh milk. We also had a churn and were able to enjoy home-produced buttermilk and fresh butter. Those were relative luxuries in those days.

Because I lived so near to school, I was able to have lunch at home. When I saw how poor the lunches were for so many of the other children, I was aware of how relatively fortunate we were. Many of the kids in school had to go to local charities to get some overalls to wear to school.

Many of my schoolmates brought their modest lunches to school. The kids who travelled on the school bus had their lunches in the school boiler room, converted by the school principal into a soup kitchen for the children. They could get a cup of soup or hot chocolate for a nickel for lunch.

It was not easy living in those early days, but we survived. We were taught to be thankful for what we had, even in lean times. A favorite saying in our home was: "Count your blessings one by one. You'll be amazed what the Lord has done."

After my Grandmother's death in 1929, my Grandfather and Uncle Raymond were living alone in the house built by my great-grandfather, Sam Humber, on McReynolds Street. Directly across the street was the impressive mansion built in 1880 by W.T. Jones, the President of Tyson & Jones Buggy Makers, only slightly grander than Sam's house.

The house was filled with mementos of generations of our family's life and interests. In the attic was an old oaken chest

Grandfather had made for Grandmother. It was made with boards seventeen inches wide. On occasion, I liked to take a nap on that chest, and even joked later to my own children that I planned to be buried in it.

There were clothes that we'd outgrown and discarded toys from our childhood. Uncle Raymond was an enthusiastic baseball fan - an avid follower of the Philadelphia Phillies. He collected baseball cards that were included in cigarette packages in those days. Years later, my parents decided to let the house to renters, who were supposedly restricted to the ground floor only. But the kids among the families of renters somehow managed to invade the attic, and many things that we kept for safekeeping went missing. I've often wondered what those old baseball cards might fetch today.

There was ample space in the house, but suddenly no one to care for Granddad and Raymond. The big house was just too much for Granddad to manage alone. He approached Dad with a proposal that would dramatically change the family's living situation.

The family had been living in a small apartment down the street, about seven doors from Granddad.

Granddad suggested that, if Dad agreed to provide care for him and for Uncle Raymond, he would deed the house to Dad. Granddad thought it good sense for the family to consolidate households.

Dad agreed to the arrangement. But, while we ended up living in a much bigger house, the size of the combined household expanded commensurately.

As Mother's illness worsened, her ability to tend to the children was further compromised. She was, by then, completely bedbound, and needed more help to care for the larger extended family.

Dad had a widowed first cousin, named Katherine Owens, whose husband had been killed in a train accident. After his death, she was living with her sister, and earned a modest living as a caretaker for elderly or infirmed patients. As Mother's situation grew more tenuous, Katherine agreed to move into our house to help tend to Mother.

"Cousin Kate," as we called her, was a Godsend. She not only looked after Mother but provided caring and an understanding discipline to us children. When one of us misbehaved, she'd sit us in a chair, hand us a Bible and tell the offender to read Scripture, "until your father comes home." In those punitive situations, reading the Bible usually meant pretending to read the Bible, staring at it while waiting impatiently for Dad to return to offer a mild scolding.

By late 1934, Shockley, Hazelanne and I shared a bedroom. Shockley and I slept in the same large bed, while little Hazelanne slept alone across the room in a twin bed.

As with most large families sharing the same house, the close quarters created moments of competition. But we also had moments of great fun and played games among the three of us.

We had to pass nightly through Mother's bedroom to get to our quarters in the back bedroom. On one night in December 1934, the three of us were playing games and clowning around a bit. The Holidays were winding down, but we were still enjoying the playfulness of the season. New Year's Eve was just days away.

Mother was fast asleep in her bed. It was a nightly routine among the children that we would all stop by Mother's room and give her a kiss goodnight before turning in for the night. But we always made certain to remain quiet around Mother's room in order not to disturb her rest.

On this night, I was especially anxious to go to bed, and raced to get in bed before my brother and sister. I teased Shockley that I'd won the race. He made a point of mildly chastening me for not giving Mother a good night kiss. I assured him, "I'll give her a kiss in the morning."

When we awoke the next morning, we dressed and went down to have breakfast. It was December 29.

There, standing at the bottom of the landing, Dad was waiting for us. He took us all aside, wrapped us all in his arms and quietly informed us that Mother had passed away during the night.

Her death left a hole in my life.

She was a natural teacher who helped me with my lessons. She was a guide who instructed me on the proper way to behave. And on those occasions when I erred, she would gently admonish me and set me once again on the right path.

Once again, the family gathered for a funeral. There were the same sad faces among our grieving loved ones, the same solemn prayers, and rituals. But this time, I was fully aware of what had happened.

I was eight years old, and my sweet Mother was gone forever.

3

MOVING ON

Often, some of the saddest words we hear when we lose someone dear to us is that timeless refrain: "Life goes on." The words are always meant to comfort but can often ring hollow. Loss is just so very hard to process, especially for a little boy.

Yet eventually ... move on, we must.

Dad had rose vines hanging on the fence of our driveway. On one side of the fence were white roses and on the other side were red roses. They perennially bloomed near Mothers' Day. On that special day, he took roses to church and handed them to women who weren't already wearing one. He insisted that the red roses symbolized a tribute to living mothers, and the white roses to those who had passed on.

He always maintained an extra supply of roses in the vestibule of the church.

Dad remained a strong source of support for me after Mother died. He tried to lift my spirits in any way he could. When he woke us in the morning, he would greet the day cheerfully with a smile. On the first day of every month, he would wake us with a greeting from English folklore:

"Rabbit, Rabbit, it's time to get up!"

The practice originated from an ancient English superstition. Uttering the word "Rabbit" as the first word spoken each month was believed to bring good luck for entire the month. It was a wonderful bonding experience for Dad and me, and we observed the practice every month for years. I still do with my own children.

As a special treat, Dad occasionally took me fishing with him.

It could be awfully difficult to find worms for bait. We'd go out behind the house, where a creek wound through the woods. We'd dig for worms in a damp earthy spot in the chicken yard, near the creek.

Dad preferred fly fishing. He liked to cast for largemouth bass from a boat using artificial plugs. They were an excellent sporting fish, were flavorful at the table, and the daily catch certainly helped extend the family's food budget.

Meanwhile, I would position myself behind the old mill and fish for perch. At the end of the day, Dad would have two or three big bass, while I'd have a string of perch.

If we'd had a good haul, he'd have me call the local preacher, with whom we'd share our catch.

Interestingly, a few years later, we spotted an ad in the local newspaper for baitworms raised by Carters Worm Ranch, in Plains, Georgia. The business was run by the same family that would produce a future President of the United States.

I ordered a small shipment of worms and was very excited to receive them in the mail. I made a cinder block enclosure, four feet by eight feet. Then, I put in a layer of sawdust and earth and chicken feed and spread over the enclosure a cover of burlap. That kept the area damp.

Over time, the worms reproduced. Whenever we'd go fishing, I'd just pull open the burlap top, reach in and grab a handful of worms.

Fishing with my Dad remains one of the treasured memories of my childhood.

Dad would sometimes let me ride with him as he delivered mail along his route.

Many of the patrons on his route lived well out of town. In those days, few had a telephone and virtually no one had a car or access to easy transportation. People were often leaving him notes along his route, asking him to pick up something.

He'd set out early after breakfast and drive the seven miles to Cameron, arrive at the Cameron post office by seven in the morning, and then start out on his mail route. He was usually able to finish in time to be home for lunch around noon.

Then in the afternoon, he'd go uptown to Carthage and do shopping for the family and for patrons on his mail route.

He was constantly running errands, helping people in any way he could.

In return, they'd give him vegetables or fruit they'd raised in the summer. Dad had a garden, as well, and he'd tell me to deliver some produce to the preacher or to some elderly neighbor in need.

He was good friends with many of the people on his route and with neighbors in town. So, they would often ask him to stop in town and pick up something from the town grocery or hardware store.

Sometimes, they'd ask him in and offer him a glass of water or buttermilk or a slice of pie, or maybe a side of mutton from the farm.

Most requests were routine, like picking up groceries or something from the hardware store. But on occasion, he'd receive a somewhat unusual request.

One day, a woman along his route asked Dad if he would be visiting the Jones Department Store in town.

Dad said "Yes, I should be near the store in the next couple of days. What are you looking for?"

"Well," she said, "I read in an ad in the paper that the store is having a sale on foundations."

"Excuse me, what?" Dad asked, "foundations?"

"Yes, you know ... foundations. Girdles, corsets, that sort of thing."

"Oh, oh, oh ... I, I, I see. Yes, yes, I, I suppose I could pick up something for you. Wha... what did you want?"

"Eldon, I'd like you to pick me up a brassiere," she said.

"Uh huh. Well, of course ... I, I, I suppose I can do that."

With that, Dad smiled nervously, said goodbye, and turned to leave.

As he raced to his car, the woman shouted cheerfully after him, "Oh, Eldon?"

"Yes, ma'am?" he answered, now anxious to be anywhere else.

"Don't forget, now, Eldon, ... size 36 D!"

On one occasion, Dad took the opportunity to teach me a lesson about showing others proper respect.

One of Dad's postal customers was a woman who did our dry cleaning. We called her "Aunt Belle."

Dad would drop off our washing and ironing with her on Monday mornings, and then pick it up on Friday after he'd finished his route. She always had a welcoming smile for us and was especially kind to me.

One day, we stopped to deliver her mail and she invited us in.

"C'mon in, Dixon," she said. "I just finished my bakin'. Sit yourself down and have a slice of my pie."

I sat down and devoured that pie, warm and right out of the oven. The sweet blueberries were just heavenly.

When we finished our conversation and returned to the car, I remarked, "Dad, that pie was delicious. Aunt Belle sure is a nice lady."

Dad answered sharply, "Don't you ever let me hear you say that again!"

"Say what again, Dad?" I asked, a bit confused.

"Never refer to Aunt Belle as a 'lady.' She's a proud woman. We will always give her the full respect she deserves."

Aunt Belle was so sweet to me on many occasions. I've never forgotten her kindness ... nor Dad's lesson in rendering respect.

Another neighbor along his route lived with his sister on a small farm where they raised pigs. Dad would occasionally send over vegetables to the family from his garden.

One day, the neighbor asked Dad to pick out two piglets for himself. The man offered to raise the pigs with the rest of the litter. In time, the litter matured, and the neighbor approached Dad and asked,

"Well, Eldon, when do you want your pigs?"

That was a big occasion. I excitedly rushed home from school on the appointed day and discovered the pigs had already been "dressed."

Nothing on the pigs had gone to waste. A wash pot was used to boil away the residual fat and render it into lard. But the real prize was the pork tenderloin we had for dinner. That was a wonderful treat in those lean days for a family struggling in the lingering Depression.

After losing my Mother, I returned to school and got back into the daily routines of lessons and games with my classmates. But, somehow, I'd lost my attentiveness and my grades suffered.

Throughout first, second and third grades, I had reliably gotten all A's. But, starting in fourth grade, my grades began to falter, and I was getting B's and C's.

Dad became worried at the downturn in my performance and visited my teacher, Frances Jane Hunter, to see what the problem might be.

My teacher explained that I'd been through a difficult time, and that it wasn't unusual for a young child in that situation to temporarily lose focus.

Dad found her explanations reassuring and paid her another visit to follow up on my progress.

Soon, he was going to see her quite often.

One day, Dad and his new school-teacher friend took us for a ride in his car. Along the way, they let us know of their plans to get married.

As is quite common in matters like these, Dad's decision to marry again was difficult for us at first.

Shockley and Hazel elected me to be the one to tell them that we didn't want Dad to get married again. While I shared their feelings, I "chickened out" when it came to discouraging the marriage.

In the long run, I realized I was right to hold my tongue. The children weren't the only ones who had suffered a loss. Dad was understandably lonely and under severe pressures as a single father. He needed help to face the future.

When news of their upcoming marriage was made known to my classmates, some of them began teasing me. "Oh, no, Dixon. Be careful. She's a redhead," one friend warned. "She's gonna give you a real rough time, all right!"

My new stepmother established some ground-rules at the outset of our new life together. She told us children that she didn't want us to call her "Mother." Instead, she said we were to call her "Mumsy." At the time, she was also my fourth-grade teacher – and took no time at all in showing that she could handle trouble.

A boy in our class was a good friend of mine. We often played with our other friends after school and had a really good time together.

Inside school, however, the boy was a very different customer altogether ... "a holy terror," in the words of his teachers.

His father was a leading businessman in Carthage and served as a civic leader in Moore County. He had a big office in the County Courthouse in Carthage.

My friend routinely sassed teachers, disturbed others in the classroom and generally did whatever he pleased. One day, he was "acting up" in his usual belligerent manner and disrupting the class.

My stepmother chastened him verbally and told him to settle down and be quiet. But the young tough kept talking back to her.

My friend continued to ignore her warnings. At one point, he turned insolent and openly challenged her.

Again, the teacher warned of possible consequences, reminding him that she kept a wooden paddle in her desk.

The boy turned to her and said, slowly and menacingly, "You must not know who my *daddy* is, do you?"

My stepmother answered back calmly, "Yes, young man, I know *exactly* who your daddy is. Now you go get that paddle from my desk and meet me in the coat room."

He gave her a defiant stare, but reluctantly walked to her desk, retrieved the paddle and went to the coat room. Whereupon she her proceeded to give the boy a severe walloping.

That appeared to quiet the boy temporarily, but he seethed inwardly throughout the rest of the day.

After school, he went home and complained loudly to his "daddy" about the spanking he'd received. His father listened, unmoved, to the boy's complaints about the teacher's "cruel treatment."

Instead, his father quietly set aside his newspaper, calmly got up from his chair and briefly left the room. When he returned, he was holding in his hands his razor strap. He proceeded to give the boy a second dose of punishment.

My Stepmother had showed that she was not someone to be trifled with.

As for my friend, it was just not a very good day to sass Mumsy.

4

ALL HANDS ON DECK

In the Depression years, money was very tight. For many families, it was necessary for everyone to pitch in when and where they could. My Stepmother was from Charlotte and was one of nine children, so we spent a good deal of time visiting the city. She was strict and a disciplinarian, but she took firm command of the family household and finances.

Shockley and I looked for odd jobs to make some spare change here and there. My Dad's new mail route originated in Cameron, about seven miles from Carthage. He made the drive early each morning. During the warmer months in late spring and early summer, he took Uncle Raymond, Shockley, and I along for the ride. Along his route there was a farm on which the owner raised dewberries.

Most people barely remember what dewberries are today. They resemble blackberries but taste much sweeter and were very popular years ago in making desserts like cobblers, jams, and pies.

Producers shipped the dewberries out from Cameron, which was the largest dewberry distributor in the world. While blackberries grow wild, dewberries are cultivated, with the vines put up on stakes.

My uncle and I managed to get summer jobs harvesting the fruit. I was nine years old. Dad would drop us off at the farm around six o'clock in the morning and pick us up shortly after noon. The son of the farm's owner was a boyhood friend, Hayes Harbour. He worked on his father's farm alongside me. Interestingly, Hayes and I were lifelong friends. Later, we ran into one another while serving overseas in the Pacific.

The berries were very delicate when ripe, so it was difficult not to crush them while harvesting. They could also be somewhat punishing, as the plants featured prickly thorns. It could be quite painful if one were not properly protected with work gloves.

Raymond was especially adept at picking the berries, delicate in handling them and efficient in packing them into his basket. He could pick eight to sixteen quarts over a morning, collecting three or four times my daily output.

We got a cent-and-a-half for every quart we picked. On a good day, Shockley and I would harvest four quarts each. We received a nickel for the four quarts. After a morning's work, we delivered our haul to the foreman. He checked our baskets and made a note of our output for the day. We each received cardboard disks, milk-stoppers, which were originally used to cover milk bottles in those days. We got colored milk stoppers representing how many quarts we'd picked for the day. Each red stopper was worth a dime; each green stopper was worth a nickel.

At the end of the week, we'd return on Saturday, turn in our milk-stoppers, and get paid. Shockley and I might get a quarter each for the week.

That was good money for a young boy in those days.

Uncle Raymond might earn two or, sometimes, as much as three dollars for the week. That really helped supplement the family budget.

When I was ten, Raymond bought me a bicycle from Montgomery Ward. I had lots of fun riding around town, visiting my friends, exploring outlying areas, and enjoying the newfound sense of independence that comes with one's first bike.

My bike also became of modest source of income for me. I ran errands for neighbors on my bicycle, and they'd give me a penny for my trouble.

While a penny wasn't a king's ransom, it was enough to buy a BB Bat, a favorite candy of mine. BB Bats consisted of taffy on a stick, either chocolate or banana flavored. I really loved the things, and just one of the sweet, sticky concoctions would last all day.

There wasn't much to do for entertainment in our little town, so we had to create our own fun. The Seaboard railroad travelled the length of the Atlantic coast, from Maine to Miami, Florida. The train didn't stop in Carthage. The nearest stop was in Cameron. There was, however, a short-line rail from Cameron to Carthage. The operator of the line would sometimes let Shockley and I ride to Cameron and back. At times, we'd watch the locomotives being repaired, or stop by the upholstery shop and watch men at work repairing furniture.

The Sears Roebuck catalog was another source of passive entertainment. Baltimore was the site of the Sears mail order house. Packages were hauled down the seaboard line to Cameron. It was fun just to look through the catalog.

For millions of Americans, the Sears catalog was a Dream Machine. A rainy day provided an opportunity to page through the catalog and see what might be within one's grasp. If Dad needed new tires or chains for his car, he ordered them from

Sears Roebuck. When I served the church in Greensboro, there was a mail order depot there. They'd have my order ready in a couple of hours.

Naturally, there was always time to play with friends. My childhood was blessed with a wide array of friends, young and old. In our neighborhood, two houses down from our house was the Methodist Church parsonage. Across the street from the parsonage was the Methodist Church itself.

There was a big house between the school and my house. An elderly man and his wife lived there. An older man lived with them and helped look after them. His name was Willy, and we chatted quite often. We were good friends for years.

Just on the other side of the parsonage was a boarding house, known as the Lang House. Living there was a Jewish family named Barron. Their son John and I were best friends all through our grade school years.

Also living in the boarding house was Mrs. McLaughlin, who cooked and cleaned for the boarders. She had a son my age named John Henry.

Every day after school, John Barron, John Henry McLaughlin, and I would play together, … roughhousing, shooting marbles, swinging from tree vines, doing the usual things that boys did for amusement.

A little creek wound its way through the woods behind our house. There was an old railroad bed left from the days when the train once travelled through Carthage. On particularly hot summer days, we'd dam up the little stream, looking for salamanders, crayfish, and tadpoles. A big grape vine hung from a tree. We cut the vine and then swung from the overhanging branches and jumped into the creek.

Sometimes, on especially hot summer days, we'd go skinny-dipping.

The three of us were the best of buddies. We didn't see the

least difference between us. Just three young boys … one Jewish, one Black, and one white Methodist.

And all having the time of our lives.

We went to visit our Great-Aunts quite often, the daughters of my great-grandfather, Sam Humber. That was a regular stop every Sunday.

Family members were clustered throughout the neighborhood. Grandmother and Granddad lived just houses away. Then, the Great-Aunts, Ada, Mame, Mattie, and Rosa. Not surprisingly, I grew up with a great respect for my elders. The consequences of any sign of disrespect could be severe. Spankings - however rare - could be quite memorable.

Aunt Mattie lived halfway between our house and the grammar school. Her grandson had a Billy Goat and a cart. He'd harness the goat to the cart, and we'd take rides around the yard. It was a real treat for the children on Sunday afternoons, pretended to be stagecoach drivers or Roman charioteers.

On Sundays, we would listen to the "old folks" talk, on the porch on balmy summer afternoons – or in the parlor in winter. It was a command performance at which we were expected to sit quietly and show respect. It was understood that we were not to speak. There, we heard - repeatedly - all the old family stories, the latest town gossip - and not a few tall tales - from the Aunts.

Before we went home, the family visited the cemetery and Dad placed flowers on the graves of his parents and that of my Mother. My Dad's little sister, who had died as a child, was buried just across the street in the Methodist Church cemetery.

One of the family's favorite stories concerned my Dad's first cousin. According to my Aunts, this cousin had done some something truly awful … utterly scandalous … simply unforgivable.

He'd gone and married a Yankee!

Sometime shortly after this news, it was announced that we were going to Aunt Mame's for a Sunday afternoon visit. This was going to be more momentous than most of our weekly visits. We were going to meet our cousin's new wife!

I was very excited about the upcoming visit. For some reason, I just couldn't comprehend what a real-life Yankee from Indiana might look like. I'd never known one, never even seen one.

On the appointed Sunday, we went over to Mame's, who lived in a big white house. In front of the house was a large, old magnolia tree that was good for climbing.

After we arrived at the house, I greeted the Aunts and then went over and hid behind the magnolia tree. There I waited until the couple finally pulled up.

Everyone was introduced amid lots of laughter and friendly banter.

Later, after all the introductions were made and everyone had their fill of Sunday dinner, I walked over to my father.

"I see you've met your new cousin," he said.

"Yes, I did, Dad ... but, Dad ... you told me she's a Yankee, but ...!"

"But what?" he asked.

"Dad," I shouted in near disbelief, "I don't understand. She's a Yankee, ... but she looks ... just like US!"

5

BORN TO BE A
PREACHER

There were three churches in Carthage when I was a boy: one for Methodists, first constructed in 1837, another for Presbyterians, built in 1851, and the third for Baptists, erected in 1859.

Interestingly, when I was growing up, there was a popular joke about religion that was making the rounds.

It seems that two friends were dozing near a creek one day, killing time on a lazy summer afternoon.

One boy asked his friend, "Now, tell me again, what's the difference between Baptists, Presbyterians and Methodists."

"Well, it's pretty simple, really," said his friend.

"All right, then, what do Baptists believe?"

"Well, Baptists believe that when you're baptized, you have to be completely submerged under water."

"You don't say! Golly! Okay, what do Presbyterians believe?"

"Ohh, Presbyterians believe in somethin' called

'pre-des-tin-a-tion.' That means anythin' that's gonna happen? ... has already been pre-arranged."

"No kiddin'? My goodness!" he said, now looking thoroughly perplexed.

"Then, what? ... what in the world do Methodists believe?"

"Methodists? Aw, shoot, that's easy," the friend said, as he pulled his hat over his eyes and turned over to resume his siesta.

"Heck, them Methodists? ... them Methodists don't believe in nothin'!"

The joke resonated with locals because religion has always been a central part of the fabric of life in North Carolina and most folks were open to some good-natured kidding.

I suppose I still remember that story because, for nearly two centuries, the Methodist Church has been a focal point of our family.

We lived just across the street from the Carthage Methodist Church. I knew the church well. My Uncle Raymond was the sexton of the church, rang the bells to announce the beginning of services on Sundays. Occasionally the basement would flood, and the fire department would come to remove the water. For all its quirks, the church was the centerpiece of our family's life.

In 1852, the Trustees of the church, who included my Great-Grandfather, Samuel W. Humber, and his future business partner, William T. Jones, oversaw the construction of a new church. The modest wooden structure had two doors facing the street, one entrance was used by women, and the other by men. Clear windows provided ample light for morning services, while kerosene lamps and tallow candles were used for evening services.

My family served the church in varied capacities for many years. My Dad's Great-Uncle, Rev. Shockley D. Adams, was a Presiding Elder in the North Carolina Conference, the equivalent of today's District Superintendent. My Dad served as Secretary of the Board of Stewards and named my brother Shockley after

Rev. Adams. Sam Humber was a church Trustee, while Uncle Raymond was Sexton.

One of my earliest childhood memories originated with my Mother. She told me - over and over again - that someday I, too, would be a preacher. That was a constant refrain in my early years.

I have no idea what made her so sure of my future role in life, but she seemed quite determined that one day I would follow a path to the ministry.

The ministry was certainly a most respectable calling, and, perhaps, she was interested in continuing the family tradition. There had been preachers in our family going back generations before the Adamses. We were descended from the Ball family in England. Reverend Richard Ball received his Doctor of Divinity degree from Magdalen College, University of Oxford in 1594.

He served as Professor of Rhetoric at Gresham College and later as Vicar at Saint Helen's, Bishopsgate, London. And, Mother's own father, Rev. Francis Ernest Dixon, was a Methodist circuit rider in eastern North Carolina for many years.

In 1894, my Grandmother, Nancy West, lived in Dover, a little hamlet in Craven County, about 130 miles east of Carthage. There were only a few hundred residents in Dover, but it was a community of devout and regular churchgoers like Grandmother.

Living in such a small community, the congregation didn't have a permanent resident minister. It was, therefore, dependent on the local circuit rider to preach on Sundays and tend to spiritual matters.

One Sunday morning, the local circuit rider came to Dover to conduct the weekly service. The air was invigorating, and the sun shone brightly under clear blue skies. It was a day made for something momentous.

As the handsome young preacher drew near in his horse-drawn carriage, he drew admiring glances from many in attendance. Rev. Dixon strode confidently to the lectern and began his sermon.

Among the admirers in the congregation was young Nancy West. She listened intently to the preacher's stirring words and was later introduced to him.

The two chatted amiably and she mentioned how much she enjoyed his sermon. She was smitten. When Nancy left the service that morning, she found herself, inspired, intrigued ... and in love.

The young people met at subsequent church services and a bond between them grew stronger. They seemed an ideal couple, drawn together by a mutual attraction and by a strongly shared faith. They began to see each other with increasing frequency, and in time, announced their intention to marry.

There was, however, a complication: Nancy was already betrothed to another man, the owner of a local general store.

Nancy and Rev. Dixon were deeply in love and remained determined to marry.

Seeing that there was no dissuading them, Nancy's father told the couple that, while he would not stand in their way, he adamantly refused to permit them to marry in Craven County.

If they were determined to wed, they'd have to do so in another county. They'd have to cross the Neuse River and get married.

They did just that. They returned home to Dover after marrying, anxious to begin their married life together. Unfortunately, another roadblock appeared.

Nancy's former suitor had threatened to sue my Grandfather for alienation of affections.

Seeking to elude any legal entanglements, the newlyweds boarded a train in Dover and travelled west to California in 1898.

They settled near Fresno, in a little town called Livermore. There, a year later, my Mother was born. She was named Gladys, after her Aunt.

While in Livermore, Grandfather spent a period serving a little church nearby.

After a year and a half in California, the couple received some welcome news: the store owner had met and married another woman.

It was now safe for them to return to North Carolina.

Once again, they boarded a train, baby Gladys in hand, and after an arduous trip east across the country, arrived safely back home in North Carolina.

Grandfather resumed his role as a circuit rider, serving Methodist churches throughout eastern North Carolina.

Methodism was to be deeply woven into the life of our family but had an unsteady start.

King James the Second attempted to return Catholicism to the English throne after the death of Charles the Second, but his efforts were rejected by Parliament. James was subsequently sent into excel.

In his place, Parliament invited his daughter Mary to assume the English throne with her husband, Prince William of Orange, the Dutch monarch.

The so-called "Glorious Revolution of 1688" returned the Protestant faith to England.

The Methodist denomination was founded as a revivalist movement within the Church of England by John Wesley and his brother Charles and others in the mid-eighteenth century.

In the early nineteenth century, the Great Awakening sparked an interest in revivalist movements and a heightened interest in spirituality. The Methodist Church experienced huge growth during that time. Much of the growth in the American Church occurred in Virginia and the Carolinas.

Itinerant preachers began traveling throughout England, visiting small villages, and gathering new followers. Immigrant preachers traveled across the Atlantic and created Methodist circuits in the colonies.

In 1784, John Wesley formally established the Methodist Church in America. The circuit rider system was very instrumental in the growth of the early church in America.

Over time, the Church in America experienced repeated splits over doctrinal matters.

From the Methodist Protestant Church there emerged two churches: the Methodist Episcopal Church South, and then the Methodist Episcopal Church North. That division was brought about by differences over the issue of slavery. Then, the Methodist Episcopal Church split over the issue of bishops. They preferred to elect a leader without bishops.

The three churches finally resolved their long-held differences and merged in 1939.

The United Evangelical Brethren Church merged with them all in 1968. The result of all those realignments is now called the United Methodist Church.

There were two conferences of the church in North Carolina, divided by the Pee Dee River that flows through the middle of the state. Everything east of the river was in the North Carolina Conference; everything west of the river was part of the Western Conference.

Grandfather Dixon served in the eastern part of the church from the 1890's through 1949. I would one day serve in the western conference from 1949 to the present. So, for well more than a century, my grandfather Dixon and I served continuously many different churches throughout North Carolina.

Consistent with Mother's plans for my future, she was insistent that I always maintain a respectful appearance. That extended to my manner of dress.

Most notably, she insisted that I wear a necktie each day to school. A tie became a regular part of my apparel. Starting in kindergarten, through grade school, into and through high school, and all the way into my college years, I was always dressed in a necktie. As the only child so attired, I was, not surprisingly, the victim of merciless teasing by the other children at school.

But Mother was very strict in our upbringing. She had strong ideas about how we should behave and was determined to set a proper example for her children. She considered my tie-wearing a sign of respect for others. Mother assured me that it was the proper attire for a future preacher.

There was another important token of my ministry. When my Grandfather died, Grandmother gave me his pocket watch, which I've treasured all my life. It was yet a reminder of our mutual paths.

6

EARLY TO WORK

Mumsy had an excellent mind for household finances and budgeting, and a good head for business. One of the first things she did after marrying Dad was to start paying down some of the debt that had accumulated during the Depression years.

She also encouraged Shockley and I to find ways in which we might help the family. After my very first paying job of picking dewberries, I had a good taste of what it was like to work in the fields.

I next moved to the tobacco fields. My first job in tobacco was "suckering." That was a task usually reserved for young boys my age. We walked through the rows of plants, picking off the hornworms that fed on the leaves.

The worms had a voracious appetite for tobacco leaves and, if left untended, they could quickly degrade the quality of the leaves, reduce the size of the crop, and in extreme cases, destroy it altogether. For doing that work, I received fifty cents a day.

One of the tobacco growers in our area was also a local barber in town. He charged thirty-five cents for a haircut. Sometimes, he'd pay me just fifteen cents cash for my work suckering in the fields and tell me to come back later and get a "free haircut."

When I was a bit older, I worked in "priming" the leaves. The lead farmer stripped the leaves off the stalk himself. He knew precisely when the leaves were at their prime point of ripeness.

The leaves at the bottom of the stalk always ripened before the top leaves. We'd pull off the smaller leaves near the bottom, which were considered less productive and thought to sap nutrients and energy from the larger healthy leaves.

From there, we placed leaves on the priming sled. A mule pulled the sled over the sandy soil and along the rows of stalks, and eventually into the tobacco barn.

Women working in the barn then "pulled" the leaves and attached them to tobacco sticks, wooden poles a bit larger than broom handles.

The women wound three or four green leaves just starting to turn from green to an orange color around the tobacco sticks in one direction, and then wrap another leaf, alternating directions.

The first signs of orange on the leaves indicated that the leaves were ready to "cure."

Adult men then climbed high to the beams that crossed the barn and hung the tobacco sticks to racks hanging from the beams. Boys my age, who did much of the field work, were not permitted to climb to the rafters.

Two large furnaces at either end of the barn were connected to large metal flues about 18 inches in diameter. When the barn was filled to its capacity, the heat was turned turn on. The temperature of the heat was gradually raised over a period of five or six days to about one-hundred and eighty degrees. The leaves were exposed to the heat for anywhere from a few days to a week or so. The steady exposure to heat removed the chlorophyll from the leaves, turning them brown. Tobacco deteriorates over time if left uncured. The smoke from the flue prevented mildew, another destructive hazard.

The leaves were then shifted to a separate room, where the women handlers removed the leaves from the sticks, and tied them into "hands," seven or eight leaves tied together. At that point, the leaves were finally ready to be sent to market.

My work in the tobacco fields normally began a little after six in the morning. Dad dropped me off on the way to the post office. Then, he'd pick me up after noon.

At my parents' urging, I saved the money I earned from my early jobs. I remember how proud I was the day I was able to buy my very first pair of overalls, feeling very much like an adult. The new overalls cost me one dollar

I also sold a local newspaper, door to door, called *The Grit*. The paper sold for five cents a copy. It cost me three and a half cents, so I made a penny and a half for every copy I sold.

The *Saturday Evening Post* and *Colliers Magazine* were also among the magazines I sold for a while. The magazine distributor dropped off the magazines weekly at the bus stop. He'd hand me a canvas bag filled with the week's latest editions of the magazines. While I only made a few pennies here and there, it helped keep me busy on those summer days.

When I was twelve, I got my first paper route. That was my first regular job.

Mumsy became the agent for the delivery and distribution of the *Raleigh News & Observer*. She did an excellent job organizing the delivery routes.

Shockley, Raymond, and I each had separate routes. I covered the west side and south side of town, Sam, the east side, and Uncle Raymond, the north side.

The papers were dropped off in front of our house, and by the time I woke, Dad had already folded the papers so that they fit in the basket of my bike. I had fifty-two deliveries to make for the morning paper and rose very early to get a start on the day. Many of my customers were farmers and early risers themselves.

For most of my route, I'd just toss the papers onto the porch, and breeze past on my bike. But some of my more demanding customers required that I place their papers inside the screen door. So, I'd have to dismount my bicycle and climb onto their porches and place the paper inside the door, slowing me down a bit.

My route took me from the Carthage Court House, over to Pinehurst Drive and then up a mile. From there, I rode back down to the Court House and up the street parallel to Pinehurst for another mile and back. In total, the morning trip was five miles. I did an awful lot of bicycle riding in those days.

I usually made it back home by six o'clock, and Dad would have breakfast waiting for me, before he left for Cameron.

Occasionally, a customer would leave out items on the porch, like hairdryers, record players or small appliances for me to fix. They knew I had an affinity for that kind of repair work. It was a way for me to earn a bit of money to supplement my modest paper route income.

After school, I delivered twenty-six papers for the afternoon *Raleigh Times*. The bus from Raleigh arrived at four pm and dropped off the papers. I'd then get back on my bike again and deliver to my afternoon customers. I collected from all my customers on Saturdays.

The subscription price for the week was twenty cents a week. I received a dollar a week for my deliveries, and an extra ten percent of all that I collected for collecting subscription fees for all my routes on Saturday.

By 1938, I was aggressively looking for work opportunities and became quite proficient at finding it. I passed by the drug store and the post office every morning on my way to school.

The local drug store was run by a genial man named Joe Allen. The store had a soda fountain, a pharmacy section and the standard array of toiletries, magazines and "notions."

At the end of the week, Mr. Allen always had an inventory of magazines that hadn't sold. He was required to return the front covers of the unsold issues to the distributor to get return credits for the unsold issues.

He let me remove the old magazines from the shelves and detach the covers, and in return I got to keep any magazines I wanted, including comic books like Superman and Dick Tracy. I wasn't getting paid in money, but I got to read all the comics I wanted for free.

Mr. Allen generally worked all by himself in the drug store. He worked backbreaking hours, from eight in the morning until around ten at night.

One day, he asked me if I'd do him a favor. He wanted me to deliver a deposit to the bank. He knew that I passed the bank every day on my way to school. Looking back, it seems that Mr. Allen placed a lot of faith in a young boy to entrust him with all the store receipts.

In time, he asked me if I had any interest in working there on paid basis. And so, I started working behind the soda fountain, serving ice cream or Cokes, whatever customers needed.

On one occasion, Mr. Allen had to go out of town, and left me in charge of the entire store in his absence.

I was just twelve years old.

Some months later, I stopped by the Ben Franklin Dime Store, which was run by Miss Edwards. I was looking for a job and asked if she could use help. She said yes, the job paid twelve and a half cents an hour.

I was excited about the new initiative, but Miss Edwards told me that I'd need to apply for a Social Security card.

Wasting no time, I found a penny postcard and addressed it

to: "Social Security - Baltimore, Maryland." On the other side, I wrote my name and a note saying, "Please send me a Social Security card."

Just three days later, I received my Social Security card in the mail. The memory has stuck in my mind all these years. In that simpler time, there was no red tape, no formal application, no regulatory hoops to jump through. I still have that card and carry it on my person to this day.

One of my first tasks working at the dime store was to assemble the bikes and trikes and wagons that had arrived unassembled. I enjoyed the mechanical aspect of putting together the disparate parts and, in the end, creating something of value and utility for customers.

Another assignment was organizing and re-pricing an inventory of men's socks. While it was a bit tedious, it was certainly informative. The socks were initially priced at twenty-nine cents. They had me remove the old price tags and put on a new tag priced forty-nine cents.

Then, they had me cross out the forty-nine-cent price and write in a new price of thirty-nine cents. Thus, what appeared to the customer to be a price reduction was, in fact, a price increase! I not only had gotten a new job ... but also an early lesson in modern merchandizing.

Those lessons came in handy later in life.

Looking back, all my early jobs - from picking dewberries and working in the tobacco fields, to delivering papers on my bicycle, to manning the soda fountain in the drug store and sorting clothes at the five-and-dime - were all good learning experiences for me.

First, I learned not to be afraid of hard work or long hours. More importantly, I learned a lot about what made people tick.

7

THE JONESES

Located kitty-corner from our house on McReynolds Street was an impressive Victorian structure. The house was built in 1880 by William T. Jones, a celebrated Civil War veteran, who served as a Confederate Army officer.

Directly across from our house was the driveway where his widow, Mrs. Jones, parked her car. To the left was her house, known popularly around town as the Jones Mansion. On the other side of the house was the cemetery for the Carthage Methodist Church, and next door, the Church itself.

Prior to the war, Jones had worked as a carriage trimmer, and was asked by Thomas B. Tyson to come work for his new company in 1857. Jones agreed to work with Tyson and brought with him a talented carriage trimmer named Samuel W. Humber, my Great-Grandfather. By 1859, the company was known as Tyson, Kelly, and Co. The company fared very well for a while, but a brief two years later, the War intervened.

Mr. Jones managed to return from Union imprisonment following the war with enough money to recommence operations at the carriage factory, which had shut down during the war.

Samuel Washington Humber was born in 1838, in Brunswick, Virginia. While his father, Oliver P. Humber, was re-settling the family in Greenville, North Carolina, Sam lived with his Aunt, Polly Finch, together with his siblings Charlotte and William. As an adult, Sam lived in Carthage, where, in 1860 at age twenty-two, he married Rosanna Cole, who was just fifteen at the time. Sam was working as a mechanic at a buggy manufacturing company headed by Rosa's father, William Cole.

In September 1861, at age twenty-three, Sam enlisted as a private in the Confederate infantry as a member of Company C of the Thirty-Fifth Regiment.

He was wounded in battle at New Bern, N.C. in March 1862. New Bern was considered an important target for Union troops, who were led by the famous General Ambrose Burnside. The city was the site of key railroad junctions that connected the North Carolina coast with the interior. As such, the railroads played a major role in the supply chain that provided weaponry and supplies to the Confederate Army of Northern Virginia. With the fighting taking place in low, marshy areas, the out-manned Confederate soldiers and militia were overwhelmed and had to fall back. Sam was injured in the battle but returned to duty after two months.

Just one month later, he was wounded a second time, at Malvern Hill, Virginia, a major battle of the Civil War. Union forces, led by General George McClellan, seized the advantage by positioning their forces and artillery atop the 140-foot Malvern Hill. General Robert E. Lee's Confederate forces conducted a sustained artillery attack on Union forces, but the Union forces withstood the barrage. Later that month, after recovering from his latest injury, Sam returned to duty, and was promoted to Second Lieutenant.

In one of the final battles of the War, Confederate forces fought valiantly, but were swamped by Union troops at the Dinwiddie Court House, Virginia, where Sam and the remaining members of the shrunken Confederate force were taken prisoner.

Just one week later, General Lee surrendered to Union General Ulysses Grant at Appomattox Court House, ending the bloody Civil War.

Sam was initially confined at Old Capital Prison in Washington, D.C. He was subsequently transferred to Johnson's Island Prison on Lake Erie, just off the coast of Ohio, a camp that held Confederate army officers. After signing the Oath of Allegiance to the Union, Sam was released and made his way back to Carthage.

At the outbreak of hostilities, William T. Jones had enlisted in the Confederate army in September 1861, also joining Company C of the 35th Regiment. He was taken prisoner in June of 1864 after a battle in Petersburg, Virginia, and was sent to Fort Delaware Union prison, the most notorious Union prisoner-of-war camps. At its peak population, the camp held twelve thousand Confederate prisoners.

The interned men were subject to sweltering heat and humidity in the summer, and bitterly cold winters. Food rations were meager, with a lean diet of bread or crackers and filthy water. Prisoners would put the bread in a cup of water to create a rough version of broth, but nothing really helped to alleviate the endless hunger.

The prisoners tended to congregate with soldiers from their own states. The most desperate among them worked together in hunting parties in a struggle to find rats. The vermin were not easy to catch but were one of the few available sources of protein when skinned and fried in grease. Some officers, who were more likely to have some disposable cash, could pay for better fare, including morsels of fish, a bit of beef, even coffee or tea.

Part of the Jones legend included his having reputedly made moonshine alcohol while in prison. He is said to have used bits of bread and potato peelings and other discarded food items to distill the odd mixture into alcohol.

While the resulting product was, predictably, of very low quality, the steady demand from Union prison guards and officers formed a reliable customer base.

By the time he was released from prison at War's end, he was thought to have amassed several thousand dollars. More importantly, his newly earned capital was in the form of Union currency, giving his money a huge advantage over the now-worthless Confederate currency. Jones returned to Carthage and reunited with Tyson. In time, he became President of the newly christened Tyson and Jones Buggy Company.

Sam Humber served as trimmer-foreman and bookkeeper of the company, and invested in the company, having purchased four shares at fifty dollars a share. He was listed as one of the original seven members of the Board of the Directors.

In the post-war years, the buggy business flourished, as a rebound in economic activity led to a booming demand for personal and commercial buggy use. As the post-war economy steadily recovered, more than three hundred local buggy and carriage makers struggled to meet the growing demand in North Carolina alone.

Buggies and carriages were the state-of-the-art form of transportation in the pre-automobile nineteenth century and were major contributors to North Carolina's manufacturing sector.

The Tyson and Jones company was among the leading manufacturers in North Carolina.

Horse-drawn buggies - and more ornate carriages for those

with upscales tastes- were designed for every segment of the market. A serviceable buggy could be had for less than one hundred dollars. A somewhat grander carriage would cost many hundreds more for the more discriminating consumer.

Manufacturing methods were primitive in those early days. The company would attach their finished vehicles by rope in a line and move them to a sales location in South Carolina. The process was painstakingly slow, but the building of a connector railroad line between Carthage and the main north-and-south coastal railway eventually eased the delivery of vehicles to sale.

Jones realized that he needed to modernize production and, on visits to northern manufacturers, he learned ways to upgrade his operation. He installed modern factory equipment and ramped up production. The company hired wheelwrights, trimmers, upholsterers, painters, and provided a good living for many workers in the post-Civil War years in North Carolina.

At its peak production, the Tyson and Jones company sold as many as three thousand buggies a year. However, as the century drew to a close, the buggy business flagged. Its death knell sounded in the early years of the twentieth century, as the automobile made its tentative entry onto the scene.

The buggy business had made Jones one of the city's wealthiest citizens. He became a leading light in civic affairs and a prominent member of the Carthage Methodist church.

After Jones's death in 1910, his widow, Florence Dockery Jones, lived alone in the house until her death in 1939. She was a fiercely proud and independent woman.

Situated as we were, just across the street, Mrs. Jones and I became fast friends. We had long chats on her porch, during which she told me rambling stories of her long life and tales of her interesting adventures. She grew up in Apex, about 45 miles northeast of Carthage. Her family was well-to-do.

Her father, Oliver Hart Dockery, had been a captain in the

Confederate Army, and was eventually promoted to Lieutenant Colonel. After the post-war reconciliation of the states, he was elected to Congress, as had his father before him. He was elected in 1868 and served two terms.

Only rarely would Mrs. Jones mention her husband's business pursuits, and even then, only in passing. On personal matters concerning Mr. Jones' life, she remained discreetly quiet.

I spent hours swinging on her wrap-around porch. I was spellbound by her wonderful stories. She, in turn, liked having a trustworthy companion willing to share them. Mrs. Jones told me stories about her life as a little girl during the war. A favorite tale was of her digging a hole in her yard behind her family's house and burying the family silver, jewelry, and other valuables. She said her family was determined to "hide their treasures from the Yankees."

Otherwise, her social life was very isolated, as she had very few friends, and kept mainly to herself.

Mrs. Jones had the first car in town. She rarely drove it, and mainly kept it stowed away in the garage. Occasionally, she would drive herself out to the cemetery to visit "her people."

Mrs. Jones didn't trust strangers. She wouldn't let anyone spend the night in her home. While she had day-time maids to help with her cleaning and cooking, she didn't want any live-in help.

She even went so far as to keep a loaded revolver on a table next to her bed.

I was happy to help her on occasions when she asked me to do her a favor. One regular errand was to go to the post office and pick up her mail and her Sunday newspaper. She always left me five pennies on the arm of her rocking chair as payment for my service.

One Sunday, I dropped her paper on her chair, as usual, but left the money. I thought to myself, "Gee I really don't want to take this nice woman's pennies."

No sooner had I left her house than she came hobbling across the street after me, carrying the old, knotted walking stick that had been her husband's.

She finally caught up with me. "Now, Dixon," she scolded me, "if you're not going to take my pennies, I no longer want you to get my paper for me!"

Another thing Mrs. Jones needed regularly was a ready supply of mineral water, fresh from the spring. She simply refused to drink water from the Carthage city reservoir.

There was a natural spring located in Jackson Springs, which had become a popular winter resort area. The spring was not far from Carthage. Every two- or three-weeks Dad drove us down to Jackson Springs, where we filled several large, five-gallon glass jugs - called carboys - with mineral water.

Dad placed the jugs on the running boards of his Model A Ford and pulled down a metal gate that folded down over the running boards to secure the jugs in place. Mrs. Jones was always overjoyed to see her mineral water supply restored.

After Mrs. Jones died in 1939, she left that walking stick to my Grandfather, who lived with us. Granddad treasured it and wouldn't let anyone touch it. Years later, when Dad and Mumsy retired, they moved to Charlotte. One of Mumsy's sisters had suffered a leg injury and needed a cane for support. The walking stick ended up with her, and sadly, it was thereafter lost to family history.

But those long-ago thoughts of my good friend Mrs. Jones have remained fresh in my memory to this day.

8

YET AGAIN ... WAR
APPROACHES

Like so many Southern families, mine has often been touched
by war over the centuries.

During the American Revolution, family members fought
beside state militia to liberate the young colonies from rule by
Britain. Among them was our distant cousin, General George
Washington. When I was in fifth grade, the class was discussing
a history lesson involving Washington. Our teacher, Mattie Kate
Shaw, mentioned that I was distantly related to the General, a
revelation that brought forth much "ooh-ing and aah-ing" from
my classmates.

But it was true. My great-great-great-great grandfather was
the father of George Washington. In 1747, another cousin, Dr.
George Glasscock invited the fifteen-year-old Washington to
Carthage, where the two half-cousins rode and hunted together,
with Washington reportedly having killed a deer near Carthage.

As I noted earlier, in the 1860's, my Great-Grandfather, Samuel Humber, fought in the Civil War as a Confederate volunteer, was twice wounded and eventually taken prisoner by Union forces.

And, in 1917 and 1918, my uncle – Dad's brother Hiram - served in World War One, fighting in the muddy trenches in France.

Now, with yet another war on the horizon, my brother Shockley turned seventeen and, in 1940, announced his intention to join the Navy. Dad had just bought a new car, a 1941 Buick. He put fifty thousand miles a year on his car as a rural mail carrier and needed to replace it every year.

One day in early December, we drove to Greensboro, ninety miles due west of Carthage, where a local postal facility housed the area's Navy recruiting office.

The family all waved goodbye and wished Shockley good luck. He always had a very outgoing personality. He later told us that, during the bus ride, he'd learned nearly everything about his future Navy colleagues.

Naturally, the family missed him terribly. Dad wrote him every Sunday with the family's news. Understandably, there wasn't much communication from Shockley's end. His busy training schedule kept him occupied. In addition, there were strict limits on what news could be conveyed home due to security concerns. If news of Navy convoy routes leaked to the wrong people, it could imperil a future mission. At risk were not only precious Navy personnel, but potentially the loss of destroyers or carriers, invaluable weapons in the war overseas.

After enlistment, Shockley was sent to Norfolk, Virginia for boot camp and basic training, which included instruction in seamanship, firearms, firefighting, and shipboard damage control, as well as lessons in values, teamwork, and discipline. He was then sent to the Great Lakes for advanced training, then assigned to the USS *New York*, which had been commissioned in 1914, and stationed in Norfolk, Virginia.

Next, he was placed aboard the shakedown cruise of the USS *Alabama*, the sister ship of the USS *North Carolina*. Shakedowns were meant to simulate the actions of the ship under maximum conditions to test the efficiency of newly commissioned or repaired ships. They also tested the mettle of new crews and evaluated their performance in stressful conditions. Shockley was a boiler tender manning the steam engine that powered the ship and was to spend most of his thirty-eight-year navy career stationed in the lower part of the ship.

Growing up in Carthage, Shockley knew everybody in town. He was the most naturally sociable person I've ever met. Some friends called him "chocolate," a twist on his given name. One mutual friend would repeatedly inquire of me, "Hey, Dixon, when's 'Chocolate' comin' home?" Shortly after his enlistment, Shockley acquired yet another nickname. He was now known - by shipmates, friends, and superiors alike - as "Sam." That remained his Navy moniker for the rest of his career.

I was admittedly somewhat envious of Shockley's easy amiability. One day, Mumsy took me aside and confided to me that, while Shockley appeared to make friends effortlessly, his friendships were merely superficial relationships. My friendships, she re-assured me, would be deeper and longer lasting.

During Shockley's initial months of training, he was, on rare occasions, able to come home on leave. When he did, he'd just share a brief greeting and a hug with the family, throw his clothes on his bed and then run into town and greet his friends. One of those leaves was in early December 1941.

As I was just 15, I was still preparing for my pending driver's license exam. I spent hours at a time in Dad's car, driving up and down the driveway, practicing parking and executing three-point turns.

On Sundays, we always had an early dinner. On this day, December 7, Dad wanted to give Shockley enough time to eat and then catch the bus to return from leave.

I turned on the car radio to listen to some music. Suddenly, a radio bulletin broke in to report the news that would change the world. Early that morning, planes from the Empire of Japan had attacked the American naval base at Pearl Harbor in Hawaii. That news hit the entire family hard.

Suddenly, the news brought the sobering reality of life home to us, as it did for all American families. I worried what the impact would be on Shockley.

After dinner, Shockley bade the family goodbye. We watched him walk across the lawn and down to the bus stop where he caught the bus and returned to duty.

When I returned to school the following Monday morning, the classrooms had the radio on, as President Roosevelt spoke to a joint session of Congress. Calling December 7 "a date which will live in infamy," the President asked that a formal state of war be declared between the United States and Japan.

A Declaration followed, and, two days later, Congress added Declarations against Japan's Axis allies, Germany and Italy. As the nation prepared for the onset of World War Two, there was, naturally, a slight air of excitement among the children.

However, for the adults - teachers, parents, and average citizens - it was a moment of heightened concern and foreboding, knowing what lay ahead.

I was working in Joe Allen's drugstore at the time. We kept a radio constantly tuned to the latest news from the front. We followed the course of War, troop advances, the latest developments. That was the way the entire nation tried to keep in touch with their husbands and sons abroad.

Overnight, the nation very quickly re-deployed its economy

to a war footing, and industrial production shifted from consumer activity to war preparations.

Detroit re-directed its manufacturing muscle from automobiles to the production of aircraft, artillery, Jeeps, and tanks.

The textile and fabric sectors shifted much of their efforts from ladies' fashions to turning out uniforms for soldiers and making parachutes.

And consumer appliance producers re-aligned their focus from making household appliances and luxury goods to creating ordnance and war materiel.

Although the full horror of what was occurring in Europe would not be apparent for some time, it was clear that it was no longer just a European war. Nazi Germany and its allies were a genuine menace and a threat to the entire world.

9

OFF TO DUKE

I enjoyed my high school years, a time of more serious learning and maturing and making those first tenuous steps from childhood to adulthood. There were dances and extracurricular activities and innocent dating. Studies included the usual 1940's curriculum, with classes in English, French, math, science, and social studies.

Many male students took "shop class" as an elective.

In the middle of the Depression, and for many years thereafter, shop programs offered instruction for students - mostly boys - in vocational programs, such as carpentry, auto repair, electronics, welding, and mechanics, which were sometimes referred to as "industrial arts." Young men in high school wanted to learn a craft that would provide a usable skill in any economy.

My parents insisted that I skip the shop class. Instead, they recommended that I take a typing class, thinking that it would prove a more transferable skill. In retrospect, I came to appreciate their forward-thinking attitude. My typing skills were increasingly helpful to me in the years that followed, and, in some cases, kept me out of harm's way.

Despite my added responsibilities in school, I continued to look for jobs wherever I could. I held on to my paper route as a continuing source of income. The nation's economy was beginning to rebound in the late 1930's and early 1940's, and most people were beginning to see a glimmer of hope for the future. But my entry into college was on the near horizon, and I needed to continue saving for tuition.

I plowed all my earnings into war bonds. Americans bought stamps and pasted them into a stamp book. When the book was entirely filled, it had a value of eighteen dollars and seventy-five cents. After 10 years, the bond would reach maturity and could be redeemed for twenty-five dollars. War bonds were very popular with most Americans. They inspired a patriotic impulse and a sense of supporting the boys overseas by helping finance the War effort … one stamp at a time.

While I was gradually building savings for college, I had absolutely no discretionary income at all for the things a normal teenager might want to do, like going to a movie, enjoying a frosty Cola-Cola on a hot summer day, or sharing a chocolate sundae with a date.

So, for a very brief period, I turned to crime. My crime? Embezzlement.

There were occasions when I'd be waiting for the *Raleigh Times* to arrive on the bus and a delinquent customer would approach me on the street and hand me some change in payment for over-due deliveries. Or, if I was waiting in the drug store, people always assumed that I worked there. A customer would come in to buy an ice cream and pay me directly.

Well, … on occasion … I'd "forget" … to ring up a sale. Maybe ten cents here, a nickel there. At first, it seemed fairly petty, and I kept a meticulous tally of what I owed, always with the intention of paying it back. But, as time went by, I realized that the nickels and dimes were really adding up. Eventually, I owed five dollars! That was a near-fortune in those days for a teenager, and I simply didn't know where to turn.

Finally, in desperation, I wrote to my Grandmother. My letter mentioned that I had gotten myself in a terrible bind. I asked her if she could lend me the five dollars. While I was deliberately vague on the particulars of my situation, Grandmother wondered what I could possibly be involved in. She sent me a check for the five dollars, but, in her note, pleaded with me, "Whatever you've been doing, Dixon ... please stop doing it!"

That alone was chastisement enough. I vowed to myself that I'd refrain from further filching and mend my ways forever.

I've stayed "clean" ever since.

One of my Great-Uncles lived next door to us. He owned a wholesale grocery operation. He loaded produce and grocery items onto his truck and delivered them to customers living further on the outskirts of Moore County.

In a building adjacent to his wholesale business, he also ran a retail grocery store called, "The Low-Price Grocery." He ran it for many years together with a loyal, long-time employee named Earl MacDonald, and eventually sold the store to him.

I worked there several years after school from four to six in the evening. On weekends, I put in a full day. In time, Mr. MacDonald just gave me a key so that I could arrive early and start arranging the vegetables, sweeping the floors, and generally making sure that the store was ready for customers. In time, he started giving me the combination to the store safe on those occasions when he'd be out of town for the day.

In all my jobs, I tried to have fun. But, when I was working in the grocery store, there were, not surprisingly, some customers that could be especially demanding.

There was one woman who had a reputation as something of a rough customer, seemingly impossible to please. When she entered the store, the other clerks would scatter like the wind. I'd walk right up to her at the door head-on, and greet her in a cheery voice:

"Why hello, Madame" I'd say. "And how are YOU this beautiful morning? What can we do to help YOU today?" Often as not, that would soften her mood a bit. I learned then that a little charm can go a long way.

Our high school principal knew that I passed by the town post office on my way to school in the morning. One day, he approached me and asked if I wouldn't mind picking up the mail for the school along the way. When I arrived at school, I'd drop the school mail on his desk.

I had my Grandfather's pocket watch that my Grandmother had bequeathed to me. Knowing that I had a reliable timepiece, the high school principal asked me to be responsible for ringing the school bell, promptly on the hour to signal the end of one class, and then again ten minutes later, to signal the start of the next class.

Soon, the principal was jokingly referring to me as his "assistant principal." Once again, like Mr. Allen at the drug store and Mr. MacDonald at the grocery, an adult was trusting me with added responsibilities at a very young age.

Fortunately, my high school years weren't only about classes and work. I found time to have some fun like most teenagers and participated in my share of extracurricular activities.

I was active in student government and was elected Senior Class President. In that position, I got to know most of the students well and expanded my social life. At graduation, I was awarded the school's Loyalty Medal.

Most of my dating activities in those early teenage years were centered on a youth group at the Carthage Methodist Church.

In my senior year, I started dating a girl frequently, and double-dating with other couples in the church group, usually after a prayer-meeting or some other Church activity.

One evening, one of the girls in our group borrowed her father's Buick for the ride to church. After the event, six of us piled into her car for the ride home. We were all laughing and kidding back and forth, when I saw one of the boys slip his arm around his girlfriend's shoulder.

I decided I'd follow suit and put my arm around my date.

At that, a girl in the group noticed and jokingly scolded me. "Hey, Dixon, what just a minute ... you can't do that! Remember, you're gonna be a preacher!"

Another girl chimed in, "Aw ... you go right ahead, Dixon. You can just remind people that 'the Lord moves in mysterious ways.'"

My last two years of high school were filled with the excitement of feeling increasingly like a grown-up and anticipating our futures. However, while the hard times of the Depression had eased, they were replaced by another major concern.

Those high school years coincided with the first years of the War. We read news from Europe that was increasingly disturbing. As a result, lurking in the back of those joyful times was the discussion of serious world matters. Shockley was already serving in the Navy and, day-by-day, the War was getting closer to all of us.

But for the moment, my eyes were trained on a new challenge in Durham.

I graduated from high school, on April 27, 1943. By the time I arrived on campus in September for my freshman year at Duke, the nation was in the middle stages of its long struggle.

My Mother had long ago told me that I was meant to be a preacher, but, yet, I hadn't felt a special calling to the role.

Nonetheless, I persisted in my studies. I was sixteen years old and enrolled in a program of pre-ministerial studies. I studied a range of courses, including Biblical passages, theology, the sacraments, and evangelism.

A transformation had taken place on college campuses across the nation, as young men enlisted in the military in droves. Duke had restructured its campus organization around the various training branches of the military. Civilian enrollment at Duke declined to just sixty or so students.

Trinity College buildings were divided into separate facilities for Army, Navy and Marines. Classrooms were devoted to teaching military tactics and strategy sessions. Dormitories housed enlisted men and officers, while athletic fields were used as training grounds for marching and practicing military maneuvers.

Thoughts of Shockley were never far from my mind. He travelled in many convoys escorting shipments of war materiel to Russia, an early ally of the United States in the conflict. But, even after the war, he remained somewhat tight-lipped about his War experiences.

During those years that he was away we missed him terribly. I picked up his extra chores when I returned from school to Carthage on weekends.

After the war in Europe had been won, Shockley's fleet was shifted to the Pacific. During one mission, his ship was struck by a Japanese torpedo. Our family learned, long after the fact, that he was in the fire room when the ship was hit. While the ship was badly damaged, Shockley survived unscathed.

As a young college student, I focused my energies on my studies, but, as I had as a boy and throughout my high school years, I needed to work to support my future studies.

As a boy, my parents had always insisted that I save my money. That advice was a valuable legacy that has served us well for generations. I went to Duke with four hundred dollars in savings from my boyhood jobs and appreciated War bonds. After three semesters at Duke, I still had sixty dollars left.

Initially, I got a job working in one of the college dining halls. I was assigned to a housing facility, primarily serving meals to marines. I worked an hour-and-a half long shift: one hour to bus tables, and a half-hour to eat. My meals were my compensation.

With most adult men engaged in some aspect of the War effort, I was able to find work easily. I found another job working evenings in the Dean's office, where I answered phones for the Information Department. I also worked in the doctors' dining hall at Duke Hospital, operating the dishwasher.

A friend at Duke had a job working for a candy distributor who delivered candy bars to the campus vending machines. He was nearing graduation and asked if I'd be interested in taking his place.

Always on the lookout for opportunity, I agreed. My job was to retrieve the candy from the storage closet and fill the vending machines. There were ten machines in the Student Union and another eight at the Duke Hospital. Each day, I retrieved the candy from a storage area and made the rounds of the vending machines around the campus. The machines each held sixty bars, selling for a nickel a piece.

The job merely involved delivery of a much-in-demand product to willing customers. Candy was a rare treat in those war days. Students would see me approaching the machines and swarm around, barely waiting for me to load the machines, often taking the bars right out of my hand, and tossing coins at me. As it turns out, selling candy to young people didn't present a huge marketing challenge.

For a while at Duke, I tried to sell Fuller Brushes. I was approached by a Fuller representative who suggested that I give it a try. Shockley's car was at my disposal, which helped my chances at getting the job.

The representative explained the line of wares and assigned me a territory of my own. While I tried my best, my door-to-door sales efforts were not very impressive.

One day, my boss accompanied me on one of my sales outings, and offered me a critique of my sales technique.

After watching me during a series of sales calls, he noted immediately what my problem was.

"Aww, no ...," he said. "You're doing it all wrong. You start out by killing the sale at the very start!"

"What do you mean?" I asked.

"You're saying to the customer, 'Say, madam, you wouldn't be looking for a new brush ... would you?' That's weak. Invariably, the customer's gonna say, 'Nah, I don't really need any brushes.' You're telling the customer at the outset not to buy your product!"

He went on, "What you need to do is ask the customer if she'd like a free fruit brush. Then, as you open your bag wide and dig deep to retrieve the fruit brush, you display the whole range of those beautiful Fuller Brushes. Often, she'll say, 'Hey, I like that brush there. I could use one of those!'"

I followed his advice, and soon I was and seeing much better results from my improved sales techniques and getting lots of orders.

Unfortunately, it was a different story when it came to completing the transactions. When I returned to deliver the goods and collect payment from my country customers, they were often nowhere to be found, or just didn't have money at the time. In the long run, it was just not a worthwhile venture for me.

After my third semester at Duke, in October of 1944, I turned eighteen. Like all young men of draft age, I was required to register with the Selective Service.

One of my primary school teachers from second grade had become head of our local draft board. She knew that I was studying in a ministerial program at Duke. She called me one day to let me know that, as a ministerial student, I was eligible for a ministerial deferment.

She told me that I should get the paperwork started as soon as possible. I thanked her but let her know that I intended to serve my time like other young men my age. She questioned me further and urged me to consider the matter further.

I told her that I was firm in my decision, explaining that I didn't want the deferment, lest anyone think that I'd gone into the ministry merely to stay out of the Army.

Just 10 days later, I received my Draft Notice.

10

PRIVATE ADAMS

On a bitterly cold day in mid-January 1945, I set off to join the Army. The entire family rose early to accompany me to the bus stop. The draftees were assembled in front of the same Carthage grocery store where I had worked as a boy a few years earlier. Mothers and fathers waited in their cars until the bus loaded, hoping to steal a last glimpse of their sons as they set out on their first steps to war.

The draftees were standing around smoking and chatting while nervously waiting for their names to be called. Although I wasn't a smoker myself, I jumped into the grocery store briefly and bought myself a pack of Philip Morris cigarettes, just so I'd fit in.

With a last name of Adams, I was used to my name being called first throughout school. In time, a uniformed sergeant appeared with a sheaf of papers and called out the roll. As I expected, "Adams!" was the first name called. I boarded the bus and went to sit down in the very back of the Greyhound coach. The bus quickly filled, with the draftees maintaining a silent vigil.

As the bus pulled away from the terminal, I waved a poignant goodbye to my family and cast a glance at the long-cherished buildings of my hometown. During the War years, a lot of buildings in Carthage were newly vacant. Eventually, they were converted into space devoted to the production of camouflage and parachutes for the military. I didn't know when I would next see the streets I'd walked and bicycled for so many years.

The bus ride from Carthage to Fort Bragg covered about forty-five miles, through winding, swerving roads lined by thick acreage of pine. Everyone on the bus was smoking, and I lit up a cigarette, as well. As the bus was meandering back and forth, I was bouncing back and forth with each turn. I started to gag on the thick, smoke-filled air in the bus, feeling more nauseous by the minute.

Finally, a bit green around the gills, I gave up the pretense of being a smoker and simply handed the pack of cigarettes to another one of the draftees. Before I'd even finished my first smoke, I was more than happy to be rid of them.

That was the first - and the last - cigarette I ever smoked. (Ironically, when I was overseas, I was placed in charge of the cigarette rations for the entire battalion.)

We arrived at Fort Bragg and were immediately met with shouted orders from drill sergeants, screaming at the confused crew of rookie recruits. Admittedly, my confusion had turned to a slight fear.

I was officially inducted into the Army upon my arrival at Fort Bragg. I was assigned a bunk in a long row of bunks, with a thin mattress and weak, squeaky springs. The contrast between my bunk and my comfortable bed on McReynolds home was palpable.

We spent three more days at Fort Bragg being processed and getting outfitted with government-issued gear and uniforms. We were then driven, each of us bearing an ungainly bag of gear, to a transport train that would take us to our next destination. The train inched forward to our next stop. As was typical of movements in wartime, we were given no clues about where we were headed.

We turned up next at Camp Wheeler, located just outside of Macon, Georgia, about three hundred and sixty-five miles southwest of Fort Bragg. Wheeler was to be our home for the next fifteen weeks of basic training.

On the first day after our arrival, the new soldiers were given an orientation lecture during which they were read the military bill of rights and informed about standard military protocols. The instructors explained the rules and regulations for every new inductee.

Every new inductee but me.

To my later dismay, I had to miss that meeting because I had been assigned KP. Again, having the name Adams put me at the front of the line. We slept in a long row of beds. Anyone assigned KP was ordered to tie a white towel to the foot of their bunk. Then, they were unceremoniously awakened at three-thirty in the morning to assume their duties for the day, including cleaning impossibly greasy pots and pans from the day's mess hall.

Missing that first-day orientation meeting was to cause me a lot of grief.

On the second day of basic training, I was assigned duty as a barracks orderly. (Yet, again … the name Adams.) I really had no idea what a barracks orderly was, so I reported and merely sat in the designated office waiting for someone to arrive and tell me what to do.

Eventually, an officer - a Lieutenant - entered the office. He saw me sitting there, and immediately called me on the carpet.

"What's the matter, soldier?" he barked. "Don't you know how to salute an officer?"

Because I'd missed that first day's instruction, I had no idea of the basic rules and protocols: how to salute; more importantly … *who* to salute. That was to prove an expensive lesson.

"Well, sir," I stammered, "I, I, … I was just …"

"Don't talk back to me, soldier! You just keep your mouth shut!" he said.

The Lieutenant had absolutely no interest in reasoning with me, a lowly private. Instead, he sent for the First Sergeant to deal with me, the offending recruit.

The First Sergeant assigned me a clearly punitive task. I was ordered to empty out the company coal bin. Then, I was to clean it. Then, after the First Sergeant was satisfied that I'd emptied all the coal from the bin, he ordered me to re-fill it with the coal I'd just removed. It was bitterly cold, and the work was a back-breaking, filthy task. But I learned some important facts of life about military rank and rules.

I was subsequently sent to attend a special session on the military bill of rights and soon learned what the other troops had been taught just days earlier.

But for the present, my first day in the army had not been a very pleasant one at all. One thing I did know for certain: I would remember the Un-lenient Lieutenant.

We spent the following weeks drilling and marching, refining our weapons skills and generally learning how to conduct ourselves.

In February 1945, President Roosevelt returned from a Conference in Yalta with British Prime Minister Winston Churchill and Russian leader Joseph Stalin. With the war in Europe nearing an end, the Allied leaders met in the Soviet Union to discuss final military strategies and a new post-War alignment.

Photos taken at the time showed that the President was in rapidly failing health. He returned to Washington from the

Conference, and, in March, travelled to his retreat in Warm Springs, Georgia, not far from our basic training base at Camp Wheeler.

Roosevelt's Georgia home - known as the "Little White House" - had been a favorite spot since his days of polio rehabilitation in the 1920's. He purchased twelve hundred acres of land in the area and built a modest vacation home in 1926. He gallantly "tried the waters" as a possible therapeutic for his condition, but the thermal therapy proved futile.

After being elected President, Roosevelt returned on rare occasions as a temporary sanctuary from the rigors of his job. He was preparing a speech to celebrate the planned opening of the United Nations, when, on April 11, he suffered a cerebral hemorrhage.

After lingering through the night, the President died the following day, April 12, 1945. For the first time in years, Americans had to face the reality that Franklin Delano Roosevelt was not their President. For those in uniform, their Commander-in-Chief was now Harry S. Truman.

We were still stationed at Camp Wheeler when the news of the President's death was announced.

Our battalion was chosen to participate in the ceremonies in Warm Springs. Dressed in our Class A "Dress" uniforms, we marched in solemn formation to pay respect to the fallen leader. After a round of somber ceremonies, the President's body was put aboard a train for the long ride from Georgia to his home in Hyde Park, New York.

As the train wound northward, the nation demonstrated a remarkable outpouring of grief for their beloved President.

Following the ceremonies, we returned to Camp Wheeler and continued our fifteen weeks of basic training, learning the fundamentals of how to be a soldier. Our next step would be advanced military training, in which we learned how to fight a war.

11

A SLOW BOAT
TO ALABANG

After our basic training was completed at Camp Wheeler, Georgia, it was assumed by most of us in the Battalion that we would be sent overseas to join the War in Europe.

However, during our months in training, Congress passed legislation barring the sending of troops overseas who were below the age of eighteen, unless they'd had six months of combat training. Accordingly, we were then sent to Fort Rucker, Alabama for advanced infantry training.

Just days after arriving at Fort Rucker, we received word that Congress had passed yet another bill, amending its earlier legislation. This bill dictated that troops under eighteen could, in fact, be sent overseas, but not to a combat zone. What followed was a cross-country trek across much of America. We were newly minted soldiers in search of a mission.

Thus, after a short stay of three weeks at Fort Rucker, we

were once again loaded on a troop train and sent to Fort Meade, Maryland to prepare us for an anticipated trip to Germany to join the occupation force there. While in Maryland, we were issued wool clothing suitable for the harsh European weather.

It seemed we would, at last, soon be headed for Europe to join the fray.

Not surprisingly, there was yet another change in plans. Instead of riding the train to New York to board a ship to Europe, we were again detoured, with stops in Pittsburgh, and then one hundred miles east to Altoona, Pennsylvania, as military plans remained very much in flux.

Eventually, we were put on another troop transport headed to Camp Maxie, near Paris, Texas. I later wrote home that I was finally going to see Paris!

The trip west lasted about five days, but seemed like weeks, as we rattled our way through the flat prairies of the Midwest and the tree-less vista of the Southwest.

While in Camp Maxie, we were still preparing for war, but this time, for war in the Pacific theater. We underwent an altogether different training regimen for advanced jungle training.

We were taught to shoot machine guns and bazookas. We also practiced how to blow up "pillboxes, the small, re-enforced concrete stations that were common in both the Pacific and European theaters. These small, fortified bunkers provided a measure of protection for observation and for small arms fire.

The Japanese forces were known to have built intricate webs of tunnels under their fortifications. One of the new skills we were taught was how to shoot flame throwers, intended to clear Japanese troops out of their bunkers. The thought of using such weapons on humans was a sobering one. But this was war, and it was just another weapon at our disposal.

Fortunately, it was a skill I was never called upon to use.

After eleven weeks of jungle training in Texas, we were sent to Fort Ord, California. We remained there only briefly, but it was remarkable to view the sweeping dunes and breathtaking ocean-side views along the jagged Monterey coast.

From Fort Ord, we travelled to Fort Anza, near Riverside, not too far from where my Mother was born. Fort Anza was established as a final depot for soldiers headed for the Pacific theater. At Anza, we exchanged our woolen clothes for lighter clothes more suitable for the torrid jungle climate. As a mild diversion, we ventured one night to nearby Hollywood. We visited the Hollywood Canteen, where movie stars entertained troops preparing to go to the Asian front.

From Anza, we boarded yet another troop train, and spent two days en route to Los Angeles. There we boarded the USS Leedstown for the "cruise" to the Pacific. We had hopscotched around the country, from the torrid heat of Alabama to the crowded cities of the northeast, from the southwest to the Golden West of California. Finally, we were on a ship that would take us to Asia to play our part in the War we'd only heard about from newsreels and newspapers. The tedium of our journey was replaced by a new excitement and fresh anxieties.

The trip to the Pacific took twenty-one days. There were seventeen hundred men on board, housed in bunk beds, stacked five bunks high, with barely eighteen inches between beds. I was on the top bunk, wedged into a bed consisting of metal bar frames, and covered in canvas. There was no privacy whatsoever, and the narrow accommodations we'd had in basic training seemed luxurious in comparison. This was our home for the three-week journey.

Some soldiers were assigned KP duty, food preparation and various cleaning assignments. The ship had church services on Sundays. If you sang in the choir as part of the religious service, you didn't have to pull any duties. Because I had sung in the choir at Duke, I was selected to sing in the ship's choir, and therefore escaped KP duty.

For entertainment, there was a movie shown at night. The same movie … every single night.

As I remember, the film was set in the Canadian Rockies and featured actor Randolph Scott. In time, you could see sailors mouthing the words to the film as they watched. Not until the ship reached some of the islands around the Philippines near the end of the voyage was there a change in movies. The new film was not terribly memorable, but it was a welcome break in the monotony.

And then, there were the card games going on at every hour, night, and day. I met a young man on board from Cody, Wyoming. His name was Eric Kristofferson, and he was an avid chess player. He wanted to play and offered to teach me the game. So, I spent a good portion of the three-week journey playing chess. Boredom was the main enemy aboard the ship, so focusing on learning chess was a welcome distraction. Eric was a Mormon, and he took me to his Mormon church services in the Philippines, yet another insightful experience learning about other religious practices.

At journey's end in August 1945, the Leedstown arrived in Leyte, on the east side of the Philippines, and then, for the next couple of days, circled around before entering Manila Harbor. In preparation for going ashore, we dressed in full combat gear. Then, we got the order to lower ourselves over the side of the ship wearing our full field packs - rifle and all - onto landing barges. The barges then went ashore, and as the front end of the barge lowered, troops poured into the shallow water and onto the beach.

Once ashore, we had our first exposure to the people of the Philippines. Friendly civilians were selling cocoanuts and bananas and found a ready market among the hungry troops approaching the landing site.

Not far from the landing area was a long train of old boxcars.

We heard that they were left over from use in France during World War One. We boarded the trains for our latest move, and slowly, the rickety trains pulled out. We travelled all night in the cramped box cars, no one getting much sleep.

We arrived the next morning at a little town called Alabang, about fifteen miles south of Manila. We then loaded into Army trucks and were driven to our new home base. Our unit was called the Fifth Replacement Depot. There, we were issued new equipment in anticipation of our role in the invasion of Japan. During those initial days in the Philippines, we waited anxiously, focusing on the uncertain days to come.

The Fifth Replacement Depot was primarily an entry-and-exit unit, processing the delivery of new troops heading to Japan to replace those that were being processed out. We encountered battle-weary troops, some of whom were veterans of both the European and Pacific Theaters.

The history of the Philippines during World War Two was a tragic one. Japan had long announced its ambitions to establish pan-Asian rule, and particularly lusted after the energy-rich assets of the French and Dutch colonies. Oil reserves and rubber plantations were important resources needed to establish its control over the region. Moreover, Japan viewed the Philippines as an important staging area for its attacks on Formosa, Indonesia, and Southeast Asia.

American forces established plans to defend the Philippines, but greatly underestimated the capabilities of the Japanese General Staff. As a result, the Philippine army remained ill-equipped, under-manned and poorly trained.

When the Pacific theater opened in December 1941, General Douglas MacArthur and the forces under his command were caught unprepared for the fierce Japanese aerial bombardment. Forced to fall back to the Bataan Peninsula and the Island of Corregidor, they surrendered in May 1942.

Japanese troops forced U.S. and Philippine troops to march from Bataan to Luzon - sixty-six miles, in what was ultimately called the Bataan Death March. The men were weak with starvation and fever. Those who could not keep up the pace were killed on the spot. The march ended at Camp O'Donnell, where another round of savagery and starvation began. In the end, only a third of the combined American-Filipino forces survived the march.

In October 1944, American forces launched a naval assault that liberated the Philippines, but not before a final orgy of killing and rape by departing Japanese forces.

One of my initial impressions and keenest memories of my time in the Philippines was that of the muddy terrain. We arrived in the middle of the rainy season and the downpours rarely let up. The area around our base at Alabang was a bleak landscape of dark black mud, quite unlike the red mud I was accustomed to in North Carolina. We'd have to navigate through mud with every step. It was exhausting to trudge through, and we always carried an extra pair of combat boots at our disposal.

With the heavy downpours a near-constant threat, we could never get thoroughly dry. Occasionally, the sun would break through, and we'd use those fleeting moments as an opportunity to try to dry our clothes. But those efforts were largely futile.

We were assigned occasional duties, KP, guard duty, "policing" the area and picking up debris. But mainly, we just waited ... waited nervously for the word that we were headed into combat.

Finally, we awoke early on a soggy August morning, all of us prepared to board a ship that would take us to Japan. Some preferred to keep a solitary vigil, staring blankly at the ground. Others chatted in small groups amid the sounds of nervous laughter and forced bravado. Then, after an agonizing wait, we heard the news. On the very day that we were scheduled to head to Japan, we heard the report that changed everything.

President Harry Truman had ordered the nuclear bombing of Hiroshima on August 6, 1945.

We hardly knew what to make of the reports. but events moved in rapid succession. Three days later, on August 9, Nagasaki was similarly bombed. Then, on August 15, Japan announced its unconditional surrender. The War in the Pacific was effectively over.

The reaction to the sudden end of the war was disbelief. Most troops were willing to admit their relief at the turn of events. A few, however, expressed resentment at missing their chance to get a piece of the action. I took those comments with a grain of salt.

In the end, more than twenty-five thousand American troops were killed serving in the Philippines, with many thousands more injured.

Truman's decision had saved the lives of many thousands of American lives, possibly my own. My relief was tempered by thoughts of the terrible toll suffered by the people of Japan. So many innocent lives were lost, an estimated 200,000 killed or injured in Hiroshima and Nagasaki. To this day, I am haunted by that reality ... and the tragic consequences of war.

12

MOPPING UP

When we went ashore after our initial landing in Manilla, we noticed very little damage done by the invading Japanese forces. There was the expected damage caused by war, but little sign of malicious vandalism.

However, following the Imperial surrender, all that changed. We returned to Manila and saw that the Japanese had gone on a rampage of retribution after their troops were surrounded and it was clear that they were going to be taken prisoner. After the news of Japan's defeat, Japanese forces inflicted enormous damage on the Philippines, as they had suffered a humiliating defeat and were set on exacting vengeance.

As we patrolled the villages, we were stunned at the extent of the deliberate destruction carried out, even after the war was clearly over. The modest bamboo huts of villagers were burned to the ground. Public buildings in downtown Manila were demolished. Statues were torn down and sacred religious sites and cemeteries were desecrated. Most appalling of all, enemy troops had engaged in the wholesale rape of Philippine women, an outrage that left lasting scars on countless women.

It was not merely the living who were subject to abuse. We were to encounter some truly gruesome sights.

It had long been a practice among the Filipino people to have their teeth decorated with gold fillings and dentures. It was considered a local sign of cultural pride in the display of a golden smile. The practice of gold tooth ornamentation and beautification among the indigenous people predated the arrival of the Spanish invasion in the sixteenth century.

Burial sites in the Philippines were typically situated above the ground. The people were routinely interred in mausoleums or gravesites covered with bricks or mortar to secure them during the relentless three-month rainy season.

As the Japanese soldiers went on their rampage, they engaged in widespread violation of burial sites in a depraved hunt for treasure. They dug up the shallow graves, unearthed bodies and extracted the gold fillings and dentures from corpses. The countryside was littered with severed heads and mutilated bodies found in the middle of roads and floating in lakes. It was truly an orgy of destruction. That remains an unforgettable image from my time in the war. To this day, it's the most appalling thing I've ever seen.

We faced a massive clean-up amid the stench of bodies rotting in the sweltering air of Alabang.

Oddly, these sights of brutality were in sharp contrast to the ingenious skills the Japanese displayed in the design of their fortifications. At one point, we went to Corregidor. That had been the starting point for the horrid Bataan Death March that took thousands of Philippine and American lives in 1942. The Japanese had created an intricate underground tunnel system to facilitate the undetected movement of troops. They'd even developed primitive hospital facilities to deal with their wounded. It was hard to reconcile the two scenes

With plans for our invasion of Japan now scrubbed, the mission of the Fifth Replacement Depot had changed. We now had to clean up the enormous damage, clear debris and attend to the casualties. We also had to process the huge numbers of Japanese prisoners-of-war.

Most importantly for our American soldiers and their families, we had to begin shipping our own troops back home.

Given the large number of fresh American troops that had been shipped in from the United States, the base was re-designated as a port of embarkation for return to the United States. The troop population was further swelled by the arrival of battle-fatigued men who had been fighting in Europe. Some had been in the war for five years or more with experience in France, Italy, Germany, and North Africa. The plan was to evacuate the men who had spent the longest time overseas. However, they had to wait until ships were available, and ships were in short supply.

Meanwhile, ships were slowly arriving to repatriate prisoners-of-war back to Japan.

I had been promoted to corporal and was put in charge of organizing work details around the camp. Filling out the ranks of work crews proved a challenge. Some of the veterans of the conflict in Europe were willing to take part in work details as a welcome break in the tedium of waiting for a ship home.

Others, however - those who had experienced years of hard combat - had no interest in doing kitchen or clean-up details. Quite understandably, they felt they had done their bit for the War effort, and outright refused to work on menial chores. While it made my job a bit more of a challenge, it was certainly hard to blame those men.

My next assignment was to guard teams of Japanese

prisoners-of-war, while they performed work details such as cleaning or doing yard work. I made a daily trip to the stockade and gathered a crew of twenty or so prisoners. There were no garden implements or lawn mowers at our disposal, so the Japanese were equipped with machetes with eighteen-inch blades, which they used to cut the grass.

It was somewhat disarming, at first, to be surrounded by twenty disgruntled, embittered, enemy soldiers holding potentially deadly weapons. But I was armed with a 45-automatic on my hip and a carbine - referred to as a "piece" - on my shoulder. I also reasoned that the prisoners were overwhelmingly focused on going home, and not in fighting a war that was already lost. Nonetheless, I kept my distance, and remained very watchful over my landscaping crews. The jobs went smoothly for the most part. A few prisoners even spoke a bit of English, which made communication somewhat easier.

On one occasion, I gathered a team of prisoners for the task of cleaning the Officers' Club. Happily, this time, the prisoners did not have machetes in hand. At one end of the Officers Club was the kitchen area, in the middle was the dining room, and at the other end, the officers' bar.

I had about five of the prisoners working with me cleaning the kitchen. What I realized only later was that the prisoners had been periodically switching places with each other working near the bar area. While in the bar, the prisoners were treating themselves to a quick nip of alcohol from the well-stocked bar. Then, they'd switch places again and gave another of their fellow prisoners a chance for a quick drink.

In looking back, that day at the Officers Club may well have been the high point of the prisoners' wartime experience. At the end of the workday, I marched the prisoners to the POW camp and noticed more than a few walking with a noticeable wobble in their step. It occurred to me later that I probably could have been court-martialed for the incident for my "negligence" in not spotting the tippling. Fortunately, nothing came of the matter.

The Japanese prisoners certainly weren't the only ones who liked to drink. Not surprisingly, my army buddies did more than their share of beer-drinking. They'd often kid me about my non-drinking ways and urge me to join them in the fun.

"C'mon, Dixon," they'd say, "just have a sip. If you drink enough beer, you'll grow to like it."

"That's just it, guys," I'd tell them, "I don't *want* to like it!"

Sometime later, I was assigned to a job driving a large truck that hauled trash and debris to the Alabang base trash dump. The dump was located near a steep cliff. I remember how nervous I was as the fellows working with me would yell, "Back up … c'mon back, c'mon back…" With every turn of the wheels, I was increasingly aware of the possibility that, if I wasn't careful, I might just deposit myself at the bottom of that steep cliff with the garbage. I was always quite relieved when the trash hauling was completed for the day.

Thereafter, I was assigned a job that was somewhat more interesting, but perilous in its own way.

When I was in high school my parents insisted that I take typing, thinking that it might be a useful skill later in my career. I had studied two years of Latin and two years of French. At that time, most male students added an elective course in "shop," working on cars, trucks, and heavy machinery. But my parents insisted I take typing instead.

When it became known to Battalion Command at Alabang that I could type expertly, I was sent to work in the Information and Education division of the Depot. Typing, apparently, was a valued skill in the department. Part of my job was to take dictation from news reports that were delivered over a short-wave radio. Then, I transcribed those reports into a daily, four-column "newspaper," called the "7-11 News," and then mimeographed the report, made copies, and distributed it to all the battalions in the command.

One day, I was busy working on my daily newsletter when I was visited by two or three officers who wanted to speak with me. They told me they were considering me for another position and wanted to do an in-depth interview for a job. It all appeared very "hush-hush."

As it turned out, the position involved working for the CID, the Army's Criminal Investigation Department. The unit investigated breeches of military codes and criminal activities within the Army, similar to the function of the FBI in the Federal government.

In addition to the standard interview, they conducted a battery of psychological tests and started to investigate my background more fully, as they did with all potential CID job applicants.

Shortly after the process began, I received a curious letter from Dad in North Carolina informing me of some odd things happening back in Carthage.

"Dixon," he wrote, "what in the world is going on? There have been people from the FBI running all over Carthage asking questions about you!"

I wrote him back, explaining, "I don't know what's going on myself, Dad. I'm sure you know as much as I do."

Of course, I couldn't disclose anything myself about the reason for the investigation, as the position was potentially a sensitive one. But after the investigation was completed, I was told that I had passed muster and that the officials indeed wanted me to go to work with them at CID.

In truth, I wasn't very enthusiastic about the prospect of working for the investigatory agency. I knew that the new assignment would require the approval of my current commanding officer and was hoping that he might bail me out. I was very much relieved when he met with the CID officials and refused to let me go. He'd told me on occasion that he was pleased with my work at the Information Department. Candidly, I don't think he relished the idea of having to search for a replacement. In the end, he explained to the CID that I was essential to the work of the department and that he couldn't possibly let me go.

The CID investigated criminal behavior, including all manner of black-market activities. In retrospect, I later believed that my boss's refusal to let me go may have kept me from danger. Then, and thereafter, I have always been grateful that my parents urged me to take that typing class.

Interestingly, in the course of my duties, I had noticed some very suspicious activities shortly after my arrival at the Alabang base.

I occasionally pulled guard duty on the base. The company compound was surrounded by barbed wire fencing. Troops would regularly patrol the perimeter to check for possible incursions.

Inside the perimeter of the fencing, there were streets that connected the various parts of the base. On one of the main streets was located the company PX, a store that sold provisions used by soldiers and civilians working on the base.

Across the street from the PX was a supply tent where PX inventories were stored. By far, the most valued of those inventories was a large cordoned off area reserved for cigarettes.

Cartons of cigarettes were stacked in batches covered in cosmoline, a waxy protective covering intended to keep the cartons waterproof and the cigarettes fresh. The cigarette cartons were stacked about twelve feet high, surrounded by a separate chain-link fence made of cyclone wire.

Two guards always patrolled the area. One guard walked the length of the compound until he met the other guard, then turned and reversed course until they met again in the opposite direction. A third guard was posted directly in front of the PX.

Another fence surrounded the exterior of the entire compound. The officer-of-the-day made trips in a jeep visiting guard posts to get nightly updates on any activities.

In time, I discovered that the guards had hatched a little money-making scheme.

The guard in front of the PX was serving as a watch dog for the other two. At night, the two perimeter guards met at a blind spot, which allowed them to enter, undetected, the area where the cigarettes were stored.

One guard stretched the cyclone wire just enough to allow his partner to slide into the cigarette storage enclosure. He then grabbed a case of cigarettes, then slid the cigarettes - and then himself - back under the wire to safety.

One problem with the scheme was that there was no easy way to get the stolen booty out of the compound. So, the thieves would hide them temporarily in a culvert running outside the camp.

According to base protocols, any vehicle entering or exiting the perimeter would be inspected for contents by the main gate guards.

However, if there was an officer in the truck, the gate guards simply saluted the officer and let the truck roll off the base. It turned out that one officer was taking part in the scheme.

That was how that black-market business was able to thrive for as long as it did until the perpetrators were ultimately caught and prosecuted.

I'd been warned that the unspoken rule in these quarters was to keep one's mouth shut. Otherwise, I might run the risk of being court-martialed myself.

As one officer told me in a slightly conspiratorial tone: "The way to survive in this man's army is to observe the old Japanese maxim of the three wise little monkeys:

'See no evil. Hear no evil. Speak no evil.'"

13

CULTURE CLASH

In Alabang, I had an Army friend who had been a medical student before he entered the service and was planning to return to medical school after the war. He was obviously a terribly bright fellow. I admired his choice of profession and was excited for his future. We got along quite well together, commiserated with one another about the tedium of Army life and shared stories about our respective hometowns in North Carolina.

He had told me on occasion that he wanted to take home some souvenirs with him when he returned home. I thought that was understandable, and naturally assumed he might be referring to salvaging a Japanese flag, a sword, or some other enemy fighting implement. Many soldiers wanted a keepsake to show their friends back home as a memento of what they had been through.

My friend worked in the dispensary section of the Alabang base PX, and his sleeping quarters were located there. One sunny day, I was on my way to visit him at his place of work. He wasn't in the dispensary at the time, but I was told that he was busy outside in the back of the PX.

I went out back, and as I walked out to greet him, I could see that he was tending to a small fire at the far end of the PX grounds. It looked like there was a pot positioned just above the fire. I wondered what he was up to.

I greeted him cheerfully from afar and he waved back, smiling. As I neared his location, I approached and looked into the pot. It was filled with boiling water, and emitting a sour, slightly acrid odor.

"Gee, what's that smell?" I asked.

I started to lean closer to the pot, and he held me back. "Dixon," he warned, "you don't want to breathe those fumes."

"Why, not," I asked, "what's in it?"

"Well," he explained, "the primary chemical is sodium hydroxide. You'd probably know it as lye. It's very dangerous to breathe in those chemicals."

"Then, what in the world are you doing with it?" I wondered.

"Well, you remember a while back I told you that I wanted to take home a souvenir from the war?"

"Yes, I remember. Is that it?"

"That's it," he said proudly.

I held my handkerchief over my mouth and nose and leaned ever so slightly closer into the pot. There, I discovered - to my horror - was the severed head of a Japanese soldier. The lye was intended to dissolve hair and bits of remaining flesh, as well as to bleach the skull white.

My friend had said he was determined to take home a trophy to put on his office desk. He'd made good on his promise.

That incident was yet another brutal reminder that, while the actual fighting had ended, a wartime mentality continued.

And, in wartime, men sometimes lose their minds. Savagery on both sides of the War.

After the fighting had ceased, the Army base started hiring local Filipino cooks to help prepare food in the mess halls and officers' dining facilities. We got to know civilian cooks working on the base and established collegial relationships with some. In the morning, we'd pick them up in their small villages and drive them to the base to work in camp mess halls.

One morning, as I was driving the cooking crew to the base, a large wild pig darted from the trees in front of the truck, hitting the truck broadside. The collision did a bit of damage to the truck. Not surprisingly, the pig did not survive the encounter.

When I stopped by the dining facility later, I could see the cooks already busy at work, butchering the animal.

The truck was battered. The pig was killed. But the cooks rejoiced in an unforeseen windfall.

On yet another occasion, I witnessed Filipino villagers indulge in a local culinary custom that I found both strange and off-putting.

Understandably, given the shortages brought about by the war, there was a tendency to see any kind of animal as a potential source of protein.

A group of villagers had found a stray dog. The animal was placed in a pen, and held without food, with just enough water to sustain it. After three or four days, the dog had become ravenously hungry.

A large ration of rice was then placed in the pen. Out of sheer famine, the dog devoured the rice. After the animal had gorged itself on the rice, it was then killed, placed on a bar-b-que spit, and roasted.

When it was sufficiently cooked, its stomach was sliced open. The villagers then feasted on the rice directly from the animal's stomach.

The Americans among us, who tend to treat our family dogs as beloved family members, found the practice utterly horrifying and cruel. But to those rural villagers, the meal represented a culinary delicacy. It was another awkward collision between the East and the West - a clash in cultural practices that one sometimes encounters in war.

On July 4, 1946, the Philippines were granted their long-promised independence. Not surprisingly, the day was marked by wild celebrations throughout the country, not unlike our own Independence Day holiday.

The typhoon season in the Philippines is very active in late summer, with July and August normally the peak month for storms. The Philippines took an especially severe pounding on July 6, disrupting shipping lanes, and tearing military installations to shreds. Alabang and Manilla were not spared. At one point, the typhoon's winds reached one hundred and fifty-five miles an hour. The roof of the Alabang base's housing facility was ripped away entirely.

I was working in the battalion supply building. The supply structure was partially constructed of concrete slabs, with re-enforced wire embedded within. As a result, a corner portion of the building's wall was strong enough to withstand the storm's most damaging winds. Protected in the corners of the building, we - the First Sergeant in one corner and me, positioned at another corner - rode out the worst of the gales.

When the winds finally died down a bit, we began the process of policing the area. There was a good deal of debris scattered about that needed to be cleared away, and the troops in the vicinity wasted no time in getting to work, a job that would take weeks to complete.

On July 16, in the middle of our clean-up efforts, I suddenly found myself doubled up by a sharp pain in my side. The pain was so severe that I started heading to sick bay.

"Hey, get back here, Adams!" the First Sergeant yelled, "what do you think you're doin'? Stop your gold-bricking!"

"The hell, I am!" I screamed in agony. "My side is killing me!" It was clear to one and all that I was badly in need of medical attention.

A fellow soldier helped prop me up, and with his assistance, I made my way over to the sick bay. A doctor quickly examined me and determined that I had suffered a burst appendix and that I required emergency surgery.

I was loaded into an army ambulance and driven forty miles to the Fourth General Hospital, formerly Fort McKinley, which was left over from the Spanish American War of 1898 and presently served as the headquarters of General Douglas McArthur.

I was administered a spinal block, a form of anesthesia, after which the physicians performed an emergency appendectomy.

The attendants later told me that, throughout the long uncomfortable ambulance ride to Fort McKinley, I was singing the words to the old football fight song: "I'm a rambling' wreck from Georgia Tech and a hell of an engineer!"

"Did you go to Georgia Tech?" one of the attendants later asked me.

"No," I said, "I went to Duke. But I always liked that Georgia Tech song."

The morning after surgery, while I was still convalescing, I was told to walk over to the mess hall to get my morning meal. The same thing was told to me that evening for dinner. I complied and very gingerly made my way to the mess hall. I continued to feel flashes of pain after my operation.

The following morning, I got up and set off once again for the mess hall. Soon, someone yelled and stopped me, saying "Hey, you're not supposed to be walking!" I walked back to my hospital litter, and for the next three days, was served all my meals there. It was my first experience having "Breakfast in Bed."

I was recuperating in Ward Thirteen of the Fort's hospital. There were sixty patients sleeping in two separate bed wards, with thirty patients in each and just two nurses left to oversee the entire station. The nurses were nearly run off their feet, tending to patients, checking vitals, delivering and removing trays.

As I was slowly beginning to feel a bit better, I started accompanying some of the nurses at night on their rounds. Mosquitos were as thick as thieves during the rainy season in that part of the Philippines, so all the beds in the hospital were covered with mosquito nets. I aimed flashlights and held up nets while the nurses checked pulses and monitored the blood pressure of patients.

Finally, after a few days, the attending physician declared that I was ready for discharge. "You can send Adams back to his unit," he said to the nursing staff.

But the nurses never put the paperwork through. Again, the physician made the request to release me, and again, the nurses ignored his request. I ended up staying three weeks altogether in the hospital.

The nurses later confided to me that they appreciated my help and were trying to extend my stay on Ward Thirteen.

I've always remembered fondly the dedication and kindness of the nursing staff during that period. I know they greatly helped many patients in their recovery.

One of the nurses was a Lieutenant Parker, from Amesbury, Massachusetts. She spoke with a broad Boston accent, and some of us would tease her mercilessly, especially, those of us from the South.

"Why Nurse Pah-ker," I'd remark. "Did you Pahk your cah in the yahd today?"

Nurse Parker returned the good-natured teasing with some of her own, feigning a Piedmont drawl: "Why, how y'all doin' this mawnin', Corporal Adams?"

We were not above playing the occasional prank. One day, a few of us conspired to have a laugh at Lieutenant Parker's expense. A group of us started shouting for assistance from the men's latrine located just down the hall from the nurses' station: "Help ... Help! Somebody! come help!"

Lieutenant Parker came running down the hall, seeking the source of the distress call. No sooner had she rushed into the men's room, when one of the ward patients took a broom and slipped it through the outside door handles, locking the Lieutenant in the men's room.

When she realized her imprisonment, her jovial mood shifted.

"Let me out! Let me out of here right this minute!" she shouted. "Let me out or I'll have all of you court-martialed!" Meanwhile, we were all bent over in laughter. She was soon released - a bit embarrassed - but we all had a good laugh. Even Lieutenant Parker herself - good sport that she was - eventually shared in the banter.

I remained in the hospital from July 16 through August 3, when I was finally released back to my unit.

Another nurse I got to know well while in hospital was Lieutenant Mary Ann Bradley. She grew up in Birdsboro, Pennsylvania, not far from Gettysburg. In addition to serving as an Army nurse and officer, she was the niece of General Omar Bradley. For a while, we had gotten to know one another in the aftermath of my surgery and hospital stay and formed a good friendship. We attended church together on Sundays and sometimes met in downtown Manilla to see the sights.

But our friendship was destined to be a brief one. After a while, her commanding officer called her in one day. He appeared unusually stern and issued her a mild verbal reprimand.

"It has come to my attention, Lieutenant Bradley, that you've been seen socializing in the company of an enlisted man ... a Corporal Adams."

Lieutenant Bradley nodded yes.

"I needn't remind you, Lieutenant Bradley," he went on, "of the prohibition against officers fraternizing with enlisted personnel. I must tell you that if there is any further report of this kind, you will be transferred to another camp."

Ever the professional officer that she was, she needed no further reminder. The next time I saw Lieutenant Bradley, she told me that we couldn't socialize any longer.

She was a very nice young woman and an excellent nurse who had been very kind to me and to the other patients under her care. Her brief friendship made the experience of my appendicitis episode more tolerable and much more memorable.

I returned to my unit in early August, and never saw Lieutenant Bradley again.

My experiences overseas and the sobering sights I'd seen in the Philippines made me appreciate even more the fact that I was brought up in America. I've never ceased to honor the sacrifices so many men and women made for our country.

Observing the living conditions in other parts of the world was truly eye-opening, even revolting, at times. It made me thankful for how very fortunate we are. I became even more mindful of how much I missed my family, my friends, and my wonderful hometown of Carthage.

I remember that the main form of transportation in Alabang and the small towns surrounding the Fifth Replacement Depot was the "Pony Cart," little pony-drawn carts that served as taxis for people and goods throughout the agricultural area.

You simply wouldn't recognize those places today. In January 2020, I heard that the Taal volcano near Luzon had erupted anew, with ash debris landing as far as Alabang.

I subsequently visited the Internet and came across a website devoted to Alabang. On the site were photographs showing a modern transportation system, heavily trafficked city streets with modern conveniences, and most strikingly, large skyscrapers. In short, there were all the signs of a vibrant metropolitan area.

The physical changes over decades were amazing. But they also showed the sheer healing power of time, and the ability of people to forgive, adapt and recover in a period of peace.

14

HOMEWARD BOUND

The process of sending American soldiers back home was a lengthy and complicated one.

The program was nicknamed Operation Magic Carpet. At the conclusion of the fighting in Europe, there were more than three million American service personnel in Europe alone. Because the War was still going on in Asia, hundreds of thousands of troops were shifted to the Pacific theater, while more freshly trained troops, like us, were still arriving from the United States.

Shockley's fleet was among those so assigned. During one mission, his ship saw some fierce fighting, coming under fire from Japanese destroyers. Years earlier, he'd met Frances Shea, a Navy nurse, and Lieutenant Commander from Boston. They fell in love and got married while on leave in Charlestown, Massachusetts, just one day prior to Frances's own departure for the Pacific in Guam. To some, Frances and Shockley seemed something of an odd couple: the strait-laced Navy officer from New England, and the affable, easy-going, Navy boiler-man from North Carolina.

Apparently, Frances was not the most gifted of cooks. One evening, she made a casserole for dinner for Shockley and a couple of dear friends. She set the plate down in front of Shockley, who sat and stared blankly at the dish. Frances asked him if there was a problem. Shockley stared at the plate. Her feelings hurt, Frances quickly whisked the plate away and re-positioned the offending meal ... straight down the sink!

There were a lot of men and women to process through the Magic Carpet. The evacuation was made even more difficult by a severe shortage of ships in the Pacific theater. To establish a priority for the demobilization, the military introduced a points program called the Advanced Service Rating Score. A soldier was awarded one point for every month spent in the War, and an additional point for every month served overseas. Those with War decorations or battle stars were awarded more points, with still more points awarded to those with dependent children.

Personnel with eighty-five points or more were given priority and were therefore first in line to be sent home.

Not surprisingly, my name was well down the list, so I settled in for a wait that would last many months. I continued working with the Information and Education Department, churning out the "711 News." In addition, I was working in Battalion Supply. My living quarters were located directly next to Forty-Sixth Battalion Headquarters.

The Major who headed the unit was a stern customer who'd come up through the ranks the hard way. He didn't take a lot of "guff" from anybody. He carried a riding crop as part of his everyday uniform, and I suspect it was intended to burnish his image as a tough guy. His appearance certainly left no doubt that he was a no-nonsense, professional soldier.

Soon, I was made battalion supply clerk, and moved my lodgings to the supply area. There, I prepared requisitions for replacement goods, and made a daily hour-and-a-half drive to a warehouse just north of Manilla, where I filled orders and turned in old supplies in return for new equipment.

While I was working at 46th Battalion Supply, our supply tent was a popular gathering place for friends and workmates after the workday was completed. The room featured a large rectangular table that was suitable for dining, card games, and beer drinking ... the activities that constituted the typical Army "bull session." Among the friends who took part in those sessions was a man named Ben Haas, who hailed from Charlotte. Ben was a remarkable storyteller, a raconteur of rare and varied talents. He sketched caricatures of people and told wildly entertaining stories about his time in the Army and his life growing up in North Carolina. After the War, Ben turned his efforts to writing and became a popular novelist.

Among his many gifts, Ben was a consummate practical joker. In his Army job, he worked in Battalion headquarters, where he cut orders for soldiers who were being transferred to other units or theaters, and then distributed the notices to the affected personnel. One evening, he stopped by the supply tent to join the group for some after-work camaraderie. He was carrying a sheaf of papers that appeared to be new assignment orders. The pack of orders was left open, with the names open to view.

One of our friends peeked at the exposed orders and quickly shot me a glance. "Dixon," he confided to me quietly, "it says here that you're being re-assigned to the Eighty-Sixth Infantry Division." The Eighty-Sixth was a battle-hardened corps that had experienced some of the fiercest fighting in Germany. They had been among the outfits that liberated Nazi concentration camps.

At first, I was quite shaken by the news, and immediately started preparing for my imminent transfer. I bade farewell to some of my colleagues, cleared out my footlocker, and readied myself for my departure. As my nerves were increasingly on edge, my friend Ben approached me, grinned broadly, and said, "Aww, Dixon ... I was just messing with you. You're not going anywhere, my friend."

After the War, Ben and I spent some time together in Charlotte, reminiscing about our Army days and even joking about my "transfer" to the Eighty-Sixth.

Battalion command processed troops for their return home. We directed them through all the paperwork needed to find a spot on an available ship home.

One day in June 1946, a new group of officers came in to be processed. As I was scanning the faces of the group, I immediately recognized one socializing with a group of fellow officers.

I was amazed to see an old familiar face. It was the Un-lenient Lieutenant, with whom I'd had a previous encounter during basis training at Camp Wheeler.

Just days later, the Major was busy touring the Battalion facilities, and parked his Jeep next to the supply tent, near his officers' quarters. As he passed through the facility, he told me, "Corporal Adams, I'm just going to be a few minutes here. Make sure that nobody takes my Jeep."

No sooner had he left for his office than another officer came walking up the street. Lo and behold, it was the Un-lenient Lieutenant, and he was making a beeline for the Jeep.

The Lieutenant walked up to me and said, "Corporal, I'm gonna take this Jeep."

"Oh, no, sir, you can't take that Jeep," I protested. "That Jeep is reserved for the Major. He left strict instructions that no one take it."

The Lieutenant ignored me and climbed into the vehicle, saying breezily, "I'm just going to headquarters. I'll be right back."

With that, he sped off. Just moments later, the Major returned and saw that his transportation was missing.

"Corporal Adams, I thought I told you not to let anyone take my Jeep," he said angrily.

"Yes, Major, you did," I explained. "I warned the Lieutenant that the Jeep was your's, sir, but he said he needed it to visit headquarters. He just jumped in and took off with it."

The Major's face turned beet red. He was pacing back and forth, getting angrier by the second, cussing and fussing and swinging his riding crop like a man possessed.

Soon, the Jeep returned, and from it, emerged the Lieutenant.

The Major went up to the Lieutenant and gave him a dressing-down like I'd never seen. He was swinging his riding crop down one side of him and then down the other. The Lieutenant's face blanched white with fear.

I was, by then, safely inside the supply tent. But I could hear the exchange outside quite clearly. As the Major continued to read him the riot act, I smiled to myself, chuckled quietly and - recalling my episode in the sooty Camp Wheeler coal bin - thought, "Revenge, revenge. How sweet it is."

I realized then that the adage was certainly true: "Revenge is a dish best served cold."

As the months rolled by, we worked at the routine of our jobs, but always kept one eye trained on the slowly declining points-threshold. At last, in October 1946, it reached my level, and I was notified that it was my turn to go home.

There remained, however, the matter of finding an available ship, for which demand still far exceeded availability.

On a hunch, I approached Battalion headquarters and applied for air orders, asking if there was any chance that I could be sent home by C-54 transport.

C-54 Skymasters were air transports that were sturdy and dependable aircrafts. They played a huge role in the moving of troops throughout the War. A C-54 – nicknamed "The Sacred

Cow" - had earlier been assigned to President Roosevelt as his personal plane ... in effect, the forerunner of today's Air Force One. Later, C-54s were used to send food, supplies and personnel to West Berlin during the Berlin Airlift in 1947 and 1948.

I was told by command that there were a lot of men with a higher points priority in line ahead of me waiting for air orders.

While initially disappointed, once again, fate intervened on my behalf.

Command received advanced weather reports that another powerful typhoon was heading toward the sector of the Philippines. I explained that I'd already been through a previous 150-mile-an-hour typhoon.

With the storm fast approaching, there was now a concern for the safety of the air fleet. The high winds of a typhoon were capable of inflicting enormous damage to the aircraft. There was suddenly an urgent need to remove all the planes that were stationed at Nichols Field in Manila.

I was told that if I could be ready to check-in at six the next morning, there would be room for me on the flight.

My only luggage was my barracks bag. I was ready in the morning and boarded the C-54 transport for the trip to Kwajalein Island, the first leg of the journey home.

The accommodations on the plane were quite spare, just benches on either side of the fuselage, which contributed to an uncomfortable flight.

The adventure became more intense when, about four hours into the flight, the pilot revealed that the plane had just lost an engine.

C-54s had four engines. While the plane could still fly with just three engines, the risk level was raised considerably. Thus, the news was somewhat worrisome. The pilot announced that we were going to circle back for the four-hour flight back to Manila to get a replacement engine. Along the way, the crew had to throw some of the plane's cargo overboard to conserve fuel.

When at last we landed back in Manila, it took about an hour-and-a half to install the new engine. I climbed right aboard for the next attempt, but some of the other passengers were reluctant.

"Oh, no ... no way," one reluctant troop said. "I'll wait for the next available ship. I don't care how long it takes, but I ain't gettin' back on that plane agin'."

The plane proceeded on a series of flights with intermediate stops to refuel. First, back to Kwajalein Island. A second leg flew to Guam, and finally, a third flight to Johnson Island. At Johnson, the military later stored hazardous materials, such as chemical weapons and Agent Orange, thus rendering the atoll uninhabitable. There, we encountered another little air adventure.

The landing strip at Johnson Island was quite short to accommodate a C-54 landing. It was necessary for the plane to set down at a very precise point to avoid over-running the strip and ending up in the water at the other end.

We required several passes. The plane swooped down and then aborted the initial attempt to land, before lifting up and around for a couple of additional tries. Finally, the pilot got it just right and the plane landed - safe and dry.

We spent the night on Johnson Island, and the next morning set out on the four-hour flight to Hawaii. From there, we flew the 2,300 miles to San Francisco. I had little time and no desire for sight-seeing in beautiful San Francisco. My agenda was clear: I wanted to get home. I quickly caught the long train ride back across the country.

I reached Fort Bragg on October 6, 1946, back once again where I'd been inducted two years earlier. There, I underwent a physical exam and completed the paperwork needed to process me from active service. There were thousands like me that were waiting to go through demobilization, so it became a very hurried process. Some of the physical exams were quite cursory in nature. In one exam, ten of us were gathered into a room. An officer shouted to the group, "Anybody who can't hear me, raise your hand!"

No one raised a hand. I suspect that no one ever did. On October 15, I left Fort Bragg and was placed on terminal leave. Finally, on November 30, 1946, I received my official discharge from active duty.

I remained on reserve duty for another three years. I expected to re-enlist in the Army Reserves for another term but was then in electronics school in Valparaiso, Indiana. The re-enlistment documents were mailed to my home in Carthage, where Dad put them in a drawer with other correspondence awaiting my return home. As a result, I missed the deadline to re-enlist and, as a result, was not called up in 1950, when the Korean War started.

At Fort Bragg, I met a fellow soldier who worked at the base. He had his own car, was headed in my direction, and gave me a ride back all the way home to Carthage.

I arrived at the family's house quite early in the morning. Exhausted by the long journey from Nichols Field, Philippines, to McReynolds Street, Carthage, I went quietly to bed, careful not to wake the rest of the household.

No one had advance news of my arrival plans, so when I woke, the maid downstairs was alarmed by the unexpected noise coming from upstairs. I descended the stairs and saw the maid waiting there, wielding a mop in her hands that she could use as a weapon, if needed. When the household realized that the "intruder" was a friendly face, they all embraced me, and we had a happy and long-awaited reunion.

As we caught up with family news, I was surprised to learn the extent of the family's lingering financial debts. There were sizable grocery debts from the Depression that had remained for years. In addition, Dad had not yet been able to eliminate the debt from my Mother's funeral expenses from 1934. It was quite a burden during that period to have two major debts hanging over the family. Nonetheless, we were determined to honor those obligations. I used some of my mustering-out pay, plus money I'd saved from War bonds, and directed those funds toward the debt.

When the ends of the Wars in Europe and the Pacific were first announced, the nation engaged in jubilant public demonstrations, in Times Square and other raucous gatherings.

In contrast, the welcoming in small hometowns across the country was more muted ... but certainly no less joyful. Soldiers and sailors and their families and friends were overcome with happiness. They acknowledged the past sacrifices, but focused on the future, on resuming anew the life they so treasured. At last, the boys were safely home.

This boy was safely home.

Pioneering the road ahead. Dixon's grandfather, Francis Ernest Dixon, was a "Circuit Rider," serving congregations throughout eastern North Carolina.

Dixon's parents. While working at Page Trust, his banker father met Gladys West Dixon, a local schoolteacher in Aberdeen. They married in November 1920.

Born to be a preacher. Even as a little boy, Dixon's mother insisted his future role lay in the ministry.

After his mother's early death, Dixon's father was required to take on the role of dual parenting. Here with Dixon (top), Hazelanne (left), Eldon (right), and Shockley (bottom).

"Mumsy" and Eldon, Sr. When Dixon's studies faltered in grade school, his father sought guidance from his teacher, Frances Jane Hunter. She later became his wife and the source of family stability.

Private Adams. Shortly after his induction in 1945, a portrait of the newly minted soldier in Macon, GA.

Margery in Nursing School at Johns Hopkins in 1953. Leading to lasting happiness, Dixon missed that early bus in Washington, D.C.!

Climbing ever higher. After the War, Dixon worked a series of jobs while waiting for "The Call." Here, perched on high, he is stringing cable as a lineman for the regional Bell Telephone company.

"I just don't have time for this!" Over time, Dixon's increasing passion for bread-making became a central part of his ministry ...

Building in Bolivia. Dixon working on the foundation of a school construction project in Santa Cruz in 1978.

The Tyson and Jones Buggy Co. Dixon and his grandson, Rodger, Jr., visit the site of the nineteenth-century factory where Dixon's great-grandfather, Sam Humber, was a partner.

My Three Sons: Marge and Dixon's children in 2004. Rodger Lee Adams (b. 1960), Thornton Dixon Adams, Jr. ("Tad," b. 1957), and Neil Smith Adams (1964).

Honor Flight. In tribute to Military Veterans, Dixon and a long-time friend, Earl Pugh, visited the World War II Memorial in Washington, D.C. in 2011.

"Parson the Clown." Dixon entertained thousands of children and their parents at Shriners parades. Here, "clowning around" with his granddaughter, Margie.

All hands on deck. A multi-generational family vacation on Emerald Island, NC.

Rodger and Dixon, here at the beach. Whenever Dixon visited Rodger at his workplace, his presence never failed to jinx the office.

15

FALSE STARTS

After I returned from the War, I was delighted to be home with my family and friends. There was a good deal of re-telling of war stories and reminiscing from school days. There were the luxuries and simple pleasures of home-cooked meals with the family, sleeping in my own comfortable bed, taking regular hot showers, wearing freshly cleaned clothes, and attending regular services at my beloved old Carthage Methodist Church. In short, the very things I missed so much while I was away.

Happy as I was, I was also haunted by a few concerns. First, I needed to find a way to earn a living. Second, there was the issue of finishing my education. And third, I was still not convinced that my future lay in the ministry. Getting an answer to that last question was the real key to my future.

I returned to Duke for a while and ended up working once again in the dining hall at the Duke University Hospital, where I ran the dishwasher for the doctors' dining hall.

As a student, I regularly attended York Chapel, named for a former Methodist minister there. The Chapel had a Sunday School program, and in time, I was elected president of the York Chapel Bible Class. While there, I met Dr. Charles C. Spaulding, the head of the Spaulding Insurance Company, headquartered in Durham and the nation's largest African American insurance company.

I was becoming increasingly interested in the concept of an inter-racial ministry, and Dr. Spaulding was very supportive of the idea. We rented a house in East Durham, did some renovations, and created a modest inter-racial congregation. There was a group called Inter-Varsity that actively promoted church activities among the various colleges in the region. Bennett College, an all-Black college for women in Durham, was among the schools involved in the program. Together, we were exploring paths that supported a more diverse approach to religious activities.

I would later see an up-close example of a more unconventional religious practice in the area.

A flamboyant preacher of the period was active in the Durham area. In November of 1947, he announced plans to hold a large religious revival. He indicated, beforehand, that part of the program would involve the handling of snakes.

The announcement got a lot of people excited and swelled the ranks of the crowd, including many college students in the Durham area. There was a standing-room audience in the aisles of the church that evening. When the crowd arrived, they saw on the stage a cage containing copperhead rattlesnakes. The Reverend mounted the stage, reached into the cage and pulled out two snakes, which he held aloft over his head. In the background, guitars and banjos played music with a lively beat, lending the proceedings a carnival atmosphere.

The demonstration was apparently designed to show how the Lord would protect worshippers from harm.

From harm? Perhaps. But not from arrest.

The City of Durham police department learned of the planned snake-handling and dispatched a team of officers to the scene. Two policemen, armed with snake hooks, made their way into the church.

When the preacher saw the police entering the church, he put the snakes inside his shirt. To escape, he jumped out an open first-floor window of the church, with the two policemen giving chase.

The preacher was easily apprehended. The snakes were confiscated and sent to a lab in the main health department in Raleigh. Upon inspection at the lab, it was determined that the snakes were far from harmless. They had, in fact, been found to be venomous. Fortunately, no one was injured in the incident.

Some of the handlers, however, were charged and subsequently found guilty of violating local Durham ordinances prohibiting the public handling of poisonous snakes.

My most pressing need at the time was to find a job. I began a brief stint at the local hardware in Carthage. My Grandfather had been a carpenter and as a boy, I spent many hours watching him at work. Learning as I watched, I was very familiar with the tools and terms of his trade. Therefore, I was able to help people easily find what they were searching for in the store.

After I'd worked at the hardware for a few months, I ran into a good friend from high school. He was running a service station and asked me if I'd be interested in coming to work for him. He said he needed a bookkeeper and offered me the position.

In the immediate post-war period, Billy's business was growing very quickly. People were spending money more freely, and one of the most desired purchases for consumers was an automobile. Car sales were booming in the newly revived economy, and the improved and expanding highway system made driving much more pleasurable. As a result, there was greater demand than ever for experienced repairmen and mechanics. Remarkably, the price of gasoline was just 20 cents a gallon at the time.

Billy reported some problems in the accounting area of his business. He suspected that his salesclerks were not always ringing up the receipts they were getting from customers.

When he first took over the station, Billy's lawyer had told him that his monthly tax due would be fifteen dollars a month. Billy dutifully sent the Internal Revenue Service a check for that amount every month.

He asked me to investigate the tax issue further. When I went over the records of his sales and checked applicable tax rates, I calculated that he owed twenty-seven dollars a month. He subsequently adjusted his monthly payments.

When I wasn't busy with the bookkeeping, I often helped with the garage work.

One day, Billy decided that he'd take some time off to go to the beach. He told the crew that, in his absence, I would be the boss for the day.

The station soon started to get busy, as motorists drove in for repairs, oil changes or just to top off their tanks. Around mid-morning, a man wearing a suit and tie came into the station and identified himself as an agent for the Internal Revenue Service. He asked who was in charge, and everybody pointed to me.

The agent said he was doing an audit and needed to see the company's books. I went to Billy's office and retrieved all the station's records.

The IRS man quietly set to work and spent the rest of the day pouring over the receipts and invoices from suppliers. At the end of the day, Billy returned from his day at the beach to find the man from the IRS waiting.

He greeted the man cheerfully and got an explanation for the agent's visit.

"Everything okay with the taxes?" Billy asked.

"Well, there is a small matter I'd like to discuss with you, said the agent.

The two men retired to the office.

Suddenly, Billy's face took on a worried look. "Gee, do I owe you any money?" he asked. "I swear, I've been payin' just what the lawyer said I owed for years now."

"Yes ... well, there is a balance due," the agent explained patiently.

"Gosh! Well, tell me how much it is. I'll gladly take care it right now if I can."

"Sir, the balance due is ..." he paused, "... *seventeen thousand dollars.*"

The blood drained from Billy's face. That was more money than he could even imagine.

In the end, the IRS was understanding and quite lenient, establishing a manageable timetable for repayment. Looking back, my friend was fortunate that the error was discovered when it was. The surprise visit from the IRS agent was a blessing in disguise.

Billy later told me that he was frightened that he might lose his business ... or even worse, be headed to jail!

While working at the service station, I learned some valuable lessons that would stick with me throughout my life.

When I first saw my dear friend Harold Hipps following my return from the Army, he was busy organizing "folk games" at West Market Methodist Church. The games involved square-dancing, which Harold had taken an interest in to introduce some wholesome entertainment into his youth ministry at West Market. Many conservative churches generally frowned on dancing altogether. But the Methodist Church had produced some records called "The World of Fun," that were played as musical accompaniment to this innocent pastime.

Harold had learned how to call the dances while at Duke. He started teaching lessons, which took place in the basement of the Duke Chapel. He found his fellow Duke students very keen to learn the dance and was soon conducting classes and exhibitions at various civic organizations, such as Kiwanis, Lions and Rotary Clubs around Greensboro and Durham.

Harold's interest in square-dancing was first piqued by a 1946 movie, "Duel in the Sun." The movie starred Gregory Peck and Jennifer Jones and featured what we now recognize as square-dancing. The dances in the film were directed by Lloyd Shaw, who was considered the father of modern square-dancing, and who also had a cameo role in the film as the dance-caller.

Square-dancing is thought to have originated in sixteenth century England as a less formal version of the English court dances and the French quadrille in Paris. The dance form made its way to New England in the eighteenth century and took on its unique regional varieties in the Southeast and, ultimately, in the Western states. Shaw went on to direct square dance scenes in several other Hollywood movies with western themes.

In its most basic form, the dance involves four couples who exchange partners and form various routines in response to a "caller," who announces pre-arranged formations. The dance form in this country initially consisted of what were called "Appalachian running sets." People danced as couples, moving in response to the caller who shouted easily recognizable commands. The Number One couple danced at the head. Number Two was to the side; Number Three was at the foot; and Number Four was on the other wing. The four couples weaved into and out of formation. Over time, the dance moves became more elaborate and the commands more varied.

Shaw noticed that most dance-callers were on the older side. Afraid that the art form was in danger of being lost altogether, he created classes to introduce the form to a younger generation and pass on the skill of calling the dance moves. He is credited with having kept that folk dancing form alive in the Western states.

After I'd been volunteering in the West Market youth program for a while, Harold asked if I'd like to accompany him to the Lake Junaluska program in the summer. Lake Junaluska was the site of the annual Summer Assembly of the southeastern jurisdiction of the Methodist Church. Families gathered to socialize with friends and their children, while Church elders met in consultative sessions. Harold attended the gathering every year, teaching several classes, and developing summer recreation programs for young people. I tagged along with Harold to the beautiful retreat in western North Carolina, and lent Harold and organizers a hand in arranging games for children.

When I returned home from Junaluska, I continued my volunteer work at West Market. Increasingly, the Church was starting to employ emerging electronics in its ministries, including audio and visual equipment, slide projectors, microphones, speakers, and 16-millimeter projectors. These were infant technologies at the time, and completely alien to many people. While Harold was admittedly unfamiliar with the equipment, I'd had gained some exposure in the Army, having long dabbled in electronics, largely self-taught. Suddenly, I saw an area that grabbed my imagination.

Around the same time, I decided to take an aptitude test at Duke called the Kuder Preference Test. The exam lasted three days, several hours each day, and represented a thorough examination of one's goals and interests. The aim was to find one's proper career path, and, effectively, avoid "forcing a square peg into a round hole."

While I'd been told since early childhood that I was destined for the ministry, the results of the Kuder test suggested otherwise. My test scores indicated that my aptitudes were lowest in the literary and verbal areas generally required of an aspiring minister. Instead, it showed, I would be best suited - and happier - if I pursued an education and training in mechanics and electronic work.

I immediately began to investigate the possibilities of re-directing my education toward those areas. The best-known schools in the electronics area were the RCA School in New Jersey, the leading such institution, followed by Valparaiso Tech in Indiana.

I settled on Valparaiso, and, in September 1947, moved out to Indiana to begin my instruction. One area I found especially fascinating was the electronics of television design and signal transmission. Television was in its very early stages, but it was clear it would have a huge impact on communications and entertainment.

Those emerging technologies were going to affect lives in a way that none of us could even imagine then. By the time I completed my first year at Valparaiso, I was able to build a television from scratch.

Another benefit of my stay in Valparaiso was that I lived with a Mennonite family in town, a widow with children, whose husband had been killed in a train accident. I spent a good deal of time with the family, sharing thoughts about our beliefs and regularly attending church services with them. I learned a good deal more about the Mennonite religion and came to appreciate a faith that was based on living a simple, holy life centered on community. My experience with them in Valparaiso provided a valuable ecumenical lesson in appreciating differing faith systems

Before I left for Valparaiso the previous fall, I was approached by the director of a private camp about the possibility of working at his facility. I'd heard that he'd been active as a fund-raiser for various causes in the area and was well regarded. I agreed to work for him the next summer. Immediately after I returned home from school for the summer, I reported for work at his private eight-week camp, which was located not far from Lake Junaluska.

As a camp counselor, I helped organize games, led campfire singalongs and escorted bus trips to the lake and other local attractions. On occasion, I'd break out some of my old magic tricks, which I'd added to since my days at Duke. The children were amazed by the sleight-of-hand.

One of their favorites was the "sawing-a-man-in-half" illusion. We'd put one child in one cardboard box with his head sticking out one end, and another child in the second box, with his legs showing. We then wheeled the conveyance out onto the stage. Amid much derring-do, I'd saw the cardboard boxes in two.

It's an age-old trick, and some of the kids likely knew it well. But they always laughed uproariously. That illusion has thrilled has many generations of children and adults as well.

One of my assigned duties at camp was to oversee the camp "bank." As the kids arrived for the summer, they each generally deposited a modest sum - a few dollars, sometimes more - in the bank for safekeeping. They could then withdraw funds as they needed them. They'd write a little "check" for 15 cents or a quarter and withdraw enough change to pay for candy or snacks whenever they went on bus trips to the lakes or to the mountains. The camp also had a little store where the kids could buy candy and treats. I'd close the store at ten PM, when the campers were required to be in bed.

The person in charge of the camp finances was an acquaintance of the Camp Director from Florida. The Investor friend had convinced the Director that the camp represented a money-making opportunity. The proposition was that the Director would run the cafeteria, while his friend would handle the overall camp finances. After a while, it became apparent that the partnership was heading in a troubled direction.

One evening about two weeks into the camp session, the Director approached the Investor seeking the weekly funds for camp groceries and supplies.

"I need money to pay for tomorrow's grocery shopping," he said, in front of the assembled camp counselors.

Bewilderingly, the friend refused to hand over the funds.

The stunned Director became more insistent. "Now, you really must turn over the money. We need to get the week's shopping done so that the children can be fed!"

The Investor steadfastly refused to turn over the money.

An argument ensued, which grew increasingly heated.

Finally, the frustrated Director picked up a rock and threw it in the other man's' direction, the missile narrowly missing his head.

Now irate, the Director jumped in his car and sped into town to visit the Henderson police headquarters.

In no time, the Investor got into *his* car and drove to town himself. He headed to the police station, as well, to swear out a warrant against the Director, charging assault with intent to kill.

When he arrived at police headquarters, he learned that the Director had already sworn out a complaint against the friend for embezzlement of funds.

The two legal cases soon moved forward and, having been present when the argument took place, I was called as a material witness. Amid the disarray of management, the camp was immediately closed for the summer, and all of the children sent home to their families.

The camp nurse was the wife of a minister, and her son was a fellow counselor. She was very generous with her time and a mother-figure for the entire camp. She and her family owned a house near Lake Junaluska, about ten miles from Hendersonville. Because my presence was required in court, I suddenly needed somewhere to stay. She kindly offered a temporary place to stay for the stranded camp counselors until our role in the pending hearings was completed.

The hearing was initially scheduled for the next Monday morning in the Henderson Court House. Unfortunately, several witnesses failed to appear, and the hearing was postponed until the following Monday. The case was then postposed a second time, at the request of the prosecution.

I approached the sheriff and explained my own concerns: "Sir," I pleaded, "I need to be in Indiana for school in September. I just can't remain here."

"Well, son," the sheriff said, somewhat menacingly, "if you think you can't stick around, I can find a way to make you stay. I'll even arrange some accommodations for you," he offered, pointing to the Henderson city jail.

I decided to stay.

During our long wait for the wheels of justice to turn, our little band of counselors did a good deal of traveling through the beautiful mountains in the area. There are some stunning vistas in the mountains of western North Carolina, and we were having a wonderful time. But I realized that I was in serious jeopardy of missing the start of the next school year at Valparaiso. The school had a strict attendance policy that forbade excessive absences from classes. The likelihood of an extended court proceeding raised the possibility of unavoidable absences from school.

When the case was delayed a third time, until October, it seemed pointless to believe I could continue my studies at Valparaiso. After my appearances in court, I simply returned home to Carthage.

The whole farce had begun as an argument over a few dollars of petty cash to buy hot dogs and beans for summer campers. It had turned into a lengthy court case, ruined a summer holiday for scores of children and their families, and cut short my career in the electronics field.

Shortly after my return home from Valparaiso in the fall of 1949, I ran into an old friend I knew from high school and told him of my aborted plans for the summer and that I was looking for work. His father owned a tobacco warehouse - The Sanford Tobacco Company - that managed the tobacco allocated to the government at auction. The company needed a bookkeeper for the upcoming auction season. My friend knew that I had worked in the tobacco fields as a boy, and that I was quite familiar with the business. I gladly accepted the job.

After the tobacco had been cured and delivered to the tobacco warehouse, government graders passed through the stacks of tobacco and assigned each pile a quality grade. Reynolds, Lorillard and all the major tobacco companies participated at the auctions, setting their sights on the premium-grade leaves. However, if a given pile failed to reach its expected price from buyers at auction, it was withheld and reserved for the government. For example, if government graders graded a pile at $65 dollars a pound, and auction buyers only bid $55 dollars, one of our four Sanford floor men would put a special tag on the pile, wrap it in burlap sacking called a "Hogs Head," and immediately remove it from the floor and put it on a Sanford truck.

There were three tobacco warehouses in Carthage. The first sale was at nine AM; the second at noon; and the third at two PM. The auction process itself could be confusing and leave an untutored onlooker bewildered.

Auctioneers spoke in a quick-fire staccato fashion that reported bid prices to buyers. A popular television ad for Lucky Strike cigarettes ran for many years, featuring the rhythmic speech pattern of an auctioneer, punctuated with the tag line, "Sold American!"

The Sanford floor team needed to be alert to the price levels to protect tobacco from "pin-hookers," buyers who would try to snap up piles cheaply and then quickly try to re-sell for a profit at the same auction.

It was my responsibility to make sure that all of the government-allocated tobacco was loaded onto Sanford trucks, delivered to our storage warehouse and eventually reached its proper government owners.

I held the position until the tobacco sales were over in October. After that, I renewed my job search.

In the ensuing months, I had a series of disappointing job situations. To be sure, I was getting varied work experience and dealing with a wide range of people. But I also learned a valuable lesson: namely, that one couldn't necessarily count on potential employers to be straight with me.

My next job was at an optical lab that took precise specifications from opticians and produced finished lenses for patients' glasses. The work involved grinding, polishing, and shaping lenses.

When I was hired, I was assured that I'd be able to make plenty of overtime hours. That was the primary attraction of the job. We'd work brutally long hours, arriving at seven-thirty each morning, and staying until ten at night. We rushed orders out the door to meet the opticians' timetables.

In no time at all, I discovered that I'd been misled. Unhappily, when I received my first pay packet, there was no overtime pay enclosed.

I approached my employer, seeking an explanation.

"Excuse me," I said. "I was told I'd get overtime pay. I worked all those long days, but I didn't receive any pay for the extra hours."

"Oh, yeah," he told me, "You certainly did work very long hours on some days. But you never worked enough hours during the whole week to qualify for overtime."

The job paid just fifty cents an hour. I took my pay and left, again frustrated by a work-related matter.

By then, I was living at the YMCA in Greensboro. In mid-December, I landed a job at a distributor for auto parts. My job was in fulfillment, helping send out end-of-year orders. I was let go when the year-end orders were completed, reaching yet another dead end.

Next, I worked in the men's department at a department store as temporary help during the annual Christmas rush. In their feverish gift-giving, customers rushed around the store all day long, eagerly spending their cash. It was, as usual, a very festive time of year, and I enjoyed helping locate gifts for customers. Unfortunately, when the Holiday cheer ended in mid-January, so did my job.

I was becoming increasingly discouraged.

In late, 1951, as the Holidays were nearing, we received the sad news that the family had once again been impacted by war. My sister Hazelanne had married John Barber in 1948, a man from Winston-Salem, who was serving in Korea with his twin brother, Worth. The twins were exceptionally close. They enlisted in the service together during World War Two and fought as bombardiers, flying missions over North Africa.

Upon their return from the War, they enrolled at North Carolina State, where they both studied textiles, an increasingly important segment of the state's economy. They joined the Reserves, attracted in part by the fifteen-dollar monthly stipend given to Reserve officers. They were both commissioned Second Lieutenants, and, when the Korean War broke out in mid-1950, were among the first ones recalled to active duty.

They preferred to be assigned to the same duties. But, after a search of John's health records, it was discovered that he had suffered from polio as a child and walked with a slight limp. As a result, he was restricted from infantry duty, and assigned to service aboard a reconnaissance plane. Worth, meanwhile was assigned to a ground combat unit.

One night on patrol, Worth was struck by an enemy mortar shell, and was killed instantly. The family received news of his death on Christmas Eve, 1951.

The memory of this promising young life cut short cast a pall over the Holiday season for years to come. John abandoned his textile studies and shifted to public service, becoming Town Manager of North Wilkesboro, Wilkes County, and eventually County Administrator of Davie County. Hazel and the family moved down to Bermuda Run, near the famous golf course.

As a boy, I loved to watch the linemen working for Bell Telephone, perched in the air stringing phone wires on high. I envied the men who did that exciting work and often wished that I was one of them.

After I'd been laid off by the department store, I travelled to the West Market Church to visit Harold Hipps, seeking some words of consolation from my faithful friend. While at the church that day, I was introduced to the General Manager of the regional Bell Telephone company, who was a prominent church member at West Market. I mentioned to him in passing my boyhood fascination with the job his men did. The conversation expanded to my recent past and my possible future plans.

At the end of our chat, I was offered a position on the spot as a Bell lineman.

For the next two years, I installed cable for Bell Telephone. We strung wire along a route originating in Greensboro and heading twenty miles northeast to Stokesdale; and then another route, from Burlington heading forty miles north to Danville, Virginia.

This was a real job. I liked the hard, manual labor, enjoyed the opportunity to work outdoors in the fresh air and felt that I was helping build something meaningful.

At the time, I was still helping Harold with his classes in square-dancing at West Market. He learned of an opportunity to a Democrat stronghold. In fact, when I first registered to vote, Mumsy even warned me, "Now, Dixon, always remember this: if you don't register as a Democrat, your vote simply won't count."

The Stokes County registrar of voters was a farmer who lived about two miles down the road from our church. We drove to the farm, and his wife said he was down in the tobacco barn. As I'd worked in tobacco as a boy in the fields, then later in curing the leaves, and then finally for a tobacco warehouse company, I thought that Marge might find it interesting to see some of the tobacco process up close.

So, we drove a bit down a rut road to the barn. He came out to meet us.

"We came to register to vote," I told the farmer.

"Oh, I keep the books in the barn. I'll go fetch 'em for ya." He returned through a side door with the registration books, put them on the threshold and we signed in.

Marge registered as a Republican. I registered as a Democrat.

For years after, at nearly every polling place in the many jurisdictions we served, an election official would jokingly comment, "Oh, here come the Adamses ... two more votes that just cancel each other out."

One of the lay leaders of the church in Pinnacle owned the local grocery store and hardware store. The Town Post Office was in his building, and always assigned Post Office Box Number One to the local preacher.

One afternoon close to Thanksgiving, I had a funeral to officiate over at Trinity Church in King. On the way back from the service, I stopped by the post office to check my mail, as was my weekly custom. At the time, I still had the old '38 Chevy coupe that I'd bought in Relay from my friend Bob Smith.

When I entered the post office, I saw a young African American man I'd known slightly in the little community. In Pinnacle, everybody knew pretty much everybody else. The travel to Colorado as part of the First Conference of Directors of Christian Education. The meeting was to be held in Estes Park and Harold asked if I'd be interested in working on the conference. I was excited by the idea of traveling west and getting a change of scenery.

Harold had another reason for wanting to travel west. Lloyd Shaw had a school in Colorado Springs and Harold wanted to meet the legend of square-dancing.

I had never been to Colorado and was enthusiastic about making the trip. But I first needed to get time off from my job at Bell. Soon, I ran into roadblocks ahead.

"Well," said the woman in the Bell Personnel Office, "Any request for vacation time at Bell needs to be delivered with two weeks advance notice."

"All right," I said, "I can do that."

"Then," the woman continued, "you'll need it approved by your supervisor."

"Okay," I said, "that's fine by me."

"Then," she went on, "it needs to be approved by the Greensboro office."

"All right."

"… and then by the Charlotte office."

"Uh huh."

"… and, finally," she said with a bright smile, "by the Atlanta office. Then, you'll be all set!"

"Well, how long will that take," I asked.

"That'll take about two more weeks," she said.

"But I'll be gone by then!" I said, dejectedly. "Tell me, miss, how much notice do I need to quit altogether?"

"Ohh … well, to do that, you just need to give one week's notice."

"Is that right? Well, then, that's easier still," I said. "I'll give you one week's notice. Right now. I quit."

One week later, Harold and I were on our way to Colorado. We drove out to Estes Park, and after spending some time working to prepare the conference, we travelled to Colorado Springs. While there, we met Lloyd Shaw, who was a noted educator in Colorado, and served as Superintendent of the Broadmoor District schools.

We took some lessons from Shaw himself and subsequently even performed demonstration dances for audiences at the famous Broadmoor Hotel in Colorado Springs. Harold was very excited about what he'd learned in Colorado and anxious to impart his newly learned skills to his students back in Greensboro.

As I returned to North Carolina, I reflected on the trials that I'd been through over the past two years: disappointing jobs, short-circuited education plans, even a farcical legal entanglement. The one constant had been my friendship with Harold Hipps. He was, for me, a shining example, with his abiding faith, his enthusiasm for life and his commitment to community.

I'd listened to his wise counsel for years. Once again at home in Greensboro, he gave me some advice that would set me on the correct path. To advance to divinity school, I first needed a four-year degree. Harold urged me to return to school immediately and finish my degree.

Thus, it was fitting, I suppose, that following a period in which I'd struggled through so many low points of late, I was to find my future and renewed hope at a place called ... High Point.

16

HIGH POINT

I didn't have enough credits to graduate from Duke because I'd dropped out a year earlier. Hoping to get back on track academically, I visited High Point College, which is about seventy miles due west of Durham. The College was founded in 1924 by the Methodist Protestant Church and was known to have a highly respected pre-training program in ministerial studies. After conferring with the Dean at High Point, I was told that High Point would accept my credits from Duke. With those credits, I could finish my degree in just two semesters. I was excited by the news. It seemed that I'd turned a critical corner.

My studies at High Point proved very rewarding, as I had some exceptional instructors. Dean Lindlay of the theology department was especially noteworthy. He was an extraordinary teacher and provided me with wonderful career guidance.

Sadly, one morning after classes, the Dean went home for lunch, and while at home, died quite unexpectedly. His passing was a great loss to the College and to me personally. It was painful to lose such a good friend and a valued mentor.

Rev. Ken Goodson, the Minister of First Methodist Church at High Point, was chosen to take over Dr. Lindlay's position as Dean and his teaching responsibilities for remainder of the semester.

One day in theology class, Rev. Goodson inquired if there were any students scheduled to graduate in January. When I said I was going to graduate, he asked to speak with me after class.

He said that the Director of Christian Education was leaving First Methodist in January. After we discussed career interests, he asked if I would be interested in assuming a position at First Methodist. I considered the offer for a while and accepted the position as Director of Youth Activities at First Methodist. It was my first official position in the Church.

My duties included working with young people in the Church, planning activities, and helping organize summer camp, a natural fit as I'd had a good deal of experience in that area. One of my first assignments gave me an opportunity to teach a group of young people as they prepared for their Confirmation. We had a class of sixty young people who were eligible for Confirmation on Palm Sunday.

Dr. Goodson held a regular Vesper service each Sunday night. One week, he was called out of town, and asked me to fill in for him for Vespers. I'd obviously never officiated over one of the services, but somehow managed to put together a sermon.

When he returned from his business out of town, Dr. Goodson was approached by a layman who had attended my Vesper service. He gave me some very nice praise.

"Ken," he joked to Goodson. "You can feel free to leave town any time you like. We got to hear a *real* message last Sunday from Dixon!"

Ken got a kick out of that exchange and gained some

confidence in his new assistant. More important still, I gained some confidence in myself due to my favorable "review."

Two or three weeks later, we learned that the mother of the Minister of the South Main Street Church of God in High Point had passed away. Ken chose me to preach at the regular Sunday service in the minister's absence.

I was, understandably, quite nervous. In trying to compose a sermon suitable for the moment, I remembered a story I'd told many years earlier at a prayer meeting.

As the story went, an elderly woman had recently died. Her sons, having long ago moved out of town, were most anxious that her funeral be celebrated in her local church. However, the local church officials reported a problem. They searched high and low, but simply couldn't find her name anywhere on the church rolls.

The sons were insistent and suggested that the officials check the older historical rolls going back decades. Sure enough, they dug into the older records and found her named listed.

In my sermon, I asked the congregation rhetorically, "Now, tell me, people, do you really think you can tell if someone is a good Christian merely because her name is listed on an old church roll?"

At that, a man in the congregation stood up in the middle of the church, waved his hands wildly and shouted forcefully, "Preach it, Brother! Preach it!"

I was quite taken aback by the man's outburst and momentarily shaken, as were some of the other congregants.

But, upon further reflection, I regarded the moment as a sign that I was starting to make progress as a preacher and learning how to touch my listeners.

The following week was Easter Sunday, and I was sent by Ken Goodson to a church in Draper, a little town north of High Point. The minister there had been suffering some health problems, and I was sent there, I thought, to fill in for the Easter Holiday service.

After a fifty-mile drive to Draper in my brother's car, I knocked on the front door of the little church, and was greeted warmly, "Oh, you're our new preacher!"

I didn't pay any attention to the mistaken greeting. However, on ascending the pulpit, I was, again, quite surprised at my introduction to the congregants by a church elder. "I want to introduce you to Dixon Adams; he's going to be our new minister."

I wondered to myself, "What on earth is going on here?" But I just went on with my sermon.

After the evening service, I drove back to High Point. On Tuesday morning, I saw Ken Goodson later in the morning and mentioned the peculiar introduction I'd received in Draper.

"Dr. Goodson, I'm afraid there's been a serious mistake. The folks in Draper seem to think I'm their new preacher."

"Dixon," he said, smiling, "There's no mistake. You *are* their new preacher. The District Superintendent and I have discussed the matter and decided that, if you're going to learn to swim, it's best to throw you into the deep end of the pool. Congratulations! They're expecting you to start your new position on Saturday."

I asked Goodson pointedly, "Are you sure about this?"

"No," he answered candidly, "Frankly, I'm not absolutely certain at all. But they definitely need you to fill in."

I was nervous but overwhelmed by the new opportunity. I drove back up to Draper and arrived as expected a bit after noon on Saturday. No sooner had I parked my car when a woman - Miss Squires - ran out of the house wearing an apron and waving a handkerchief.

"Mr. Adams," she shouted, "Welcome to Draper! It's so good to meet you." As she was turning to go back into the house, she stopped and said, "Oh and, Mr. Adams? ... you have a funeral at two o'clock!"

Dashing into the parsonage, I looked around the liturgies in my bag for a suitable funeral service. The deceased man was named Archie Mayes. He was a prominent and well-respected member of the church. As I was searching through the liturgies, the doorbell rang, and a man came into the office. He introduced himself as a retired Moravian minister. He described himself as "the self-professed chaplain of Fieldcrest Mills," then one of the largest textile mills in North Carolina.

I described to the minister my present dilemma. He re-assured me, "No need to worry. I have a service all written out. You can get up in the pulpit and read what I have. The choir will sing a hymn. Then I'll recite a passage from Scripture. It'll be just perfect."

After the service, as the people filed out of the church, I received a bouquet of compliments from the congregants about the lovely service.

I was greatly relieved and gratified to have gotten through the funeral on such short notice. I also had a greater appreciation for the phrase, "thrown into the deep end."

I remained at the Draper church through the summer of 1953. With the Western Conference scheduled for October, the Draper church leaders indicated that they wanted me to stay at Draper in a permanent position.

While the District Superintendent voiced his appreciation for my work at Draper, he gave me some valuable career advice.

"If you ever intend to go to seminary to finish your ministerial studies, you should do so now," he urged me. "Otherwise, you'll be taking summer classes here and there, and, maybe even correspondence courses. I'd advise you to go to seminary now and finish your degree and advance to ordination. That will be the best path for your career."

I took the District Superintendent's advice to heart. At one point in my studies at High Point, I found one of my professors so dogmatic and authoritarian that I feared I just couldn't go on. I found myself starting to wonder if I had made the wrong choice.

I'd worked with and admired Dr. Ferguson, who taught a seminar called "Religious Emphasis." I thought the world of him when I heard him speak. I was able to obtain an internship and decided to major in Christian Education. I switched to Dr. Ferguson as my advisor, who was then heading the department of Pastoral Care.

He required that a graduate required at least a year working in a mental institution. So, I spent some time working at the Sykesville Mental Hospital in western Maryland, and later some time working at St. Elizabeth's Hospital in Washington, D.C. Those experiences - together with the time spent later at the Georgian Clinic at Emory - provided me with a good background in alcoholic treatment and mental disorders.

Thereafter, with the counsel of the District Superintendent in mind, I called Dr. Ferguson and inquired about the possibility of attending seminary. He agreed that it was the right move and said that they'd have a place waiting for me in Westminster, Maryland.

I left Draper in September 1953 and prepared for the move to Maryland.

For years, I'd been frustrated that I'd not yet received "the Call" to the ministry. I remembered a night years earlier in the Philippines while walking on guard duty and contemplating my future. Standing alone, I suddenly looked into the starry black sky and asked the Lord to send me a message.

I prayed silently, "If you really intend for me to be a preacher, Lord, please send a shooting star across the sky. Right now!"

I stared at the heavens in vain. There was no shooting star. No lightning strikes. No message. I had to wait a bit longer for the Call.

The Call did, at last, arrive in that little church on South Main Street in High Point. It came directly from the Congregation.

"Preach it, brother! Preach it!"

17

A COURTSHIP IN WESTMINSTER

On the day I was preparing to go to seminary in Maryland, the family gathered around the kitchen table for a bon voyage lunch. Mumsy made homemade vegetable soup for lunch, which was for many years my very favorite. I devoured it.

This was another notable day for the family. Once again, one of the boys was preparing to leave the homestead. Unlike previous departures - like Shockley's entry into the Navy in 1940 or the day I left for basic training in 1945 - this occasion was not filled with dread of the unknown.

My life was about to change dramatically … and for the better.

As we kidded back and forth and shared the usual family banter, Mumsy suddenly made an unexpected observation of me.

"Dixon," she said, "I don't believe you ever intend to get married, do you?"

It was an unusual remark to make on this occasion, and it left me a bit flustered. I tried to finesse the moment with a bit of humor.

"Well, Mumsy," I said, "I guess it all depends. Naturally, she'd have to be pretty special. But, I suppose, if I could ever find someone who can make vegetable soup as delicious as yours, I just might have to consider it." Mumsy appeared flattered by the reference to her soup.

"Oh … and of course," I added, "she'd have to like square-dancing." We all laughed, and my tension eased.

At that very moment, one of our neighbors walked in the back door. In our little town, it was quite common for friends and close neighbors to walk freely into the house from time to time. There was never a need to knock or ring a doorbell.

Our visitor was Epes Wallace, who had grown up in the house just next door. Epes was the middle daughter of three in the Wallace family. Her sister Peggy was the oldest and had been a classmate of mine in kindergarten. Nancy was the youngest.

Epes and I were the best of friends and spent many carefree hours in our childhood, playing kick the can, hide and seek, monopoly and checkers.

We hadn't seen one another in many years. She still called me "Little Dicky Adams." Every morning, after my Dad had left for work, I'd run around the Wallace's backyard, yelling "Hi-Yo, Silver, away! The Lone Ranger rides again!" The neighbors would tell me that I always woke them up in the morning, more reliably than an alarm clock.

We hugged and shared pleasantries. Epes was like a member of our extended family. She was in town briefly to visit with her sister. She said that she was married to a Pennsylvania man and that they worked together at the FBI in Washington, D.C.

I mentioned that I was taking the train later that evening to Westminster, Maryland to begin my studies at seminary. At that, Epes' eyes lit up wide. She said, excitedly, that she and her husband were planning to drive up to Washington later that very day. They both needed to get back to work at the FBI in D.C. She suggested that I ride with them, and I happily accepted her offer. It seemed like a great opportunity to catch up with my friend after all these years.

Later that day, we set off and spent the next six hours reliving stories of childhood hijinks, and our families' lives and losses. Along the way, we stopped in Richmond briefly to see Epes's sister, who was married to a Presbyterian minister.

When we arrived at the couple's home in Washington, they put me up for the night and made us a wonderful dinner.

I called the bus station to check the departure times for the following morning and found a bus leaving at seven-thirty in the morning.

What ensued over the next twelve hours showed how life sometimes bestows miracles when we least expect them.

Epes dropped me off at seven at the D.C. bus station on her way to work. I hoped to catch the seven-thirty bus to Westminster but, when I checked at the ticket counter, learned that the bus had already left a half-hour earlier. It appeared that the D.C. time-tables were different, and the next bus to Westminster wouldn't be leaving until one PM.

Deflated, I realized that I had no choice but to wait five hours for the later bus. I walked around the terminal, got something to eat, ducked outside for a while and took in some of the sights in the neighborhood. Finally, the hour arrived, and we boarded the bus that would take me to my future.

Bus rides can be very tedious and a bit wearing on the psyche. But I've found that riding through new towns and fresh terrain often changes the experience altogether.

This bus stopped in Baltimore to let on more passengers. There, a pretty, young woman boarded, struggling with her bag.

I jumped up and helped her stow her bag, and she sat down in the seat beside me.

We shared small-talk, and I learned that she was a nursing student studying at Johns Hopkins. She was headed back for a visit with her family in Johnstown, Pennsylvania.

I mentioned that I was going off to study at Seminary. She said that her grandfather, like mine, had been a minister, he with the Evangelical United Brethren Church. We chatted about school, our families, and our hometowns.

The ride from Baltimore to Westminster usually took about an hour, but that day the trip seemed to pass by in mere minutes.

When the bus reached my final destination at Westminster, I got up to leave, nervously mentioned how much I enjoyed our chat and bade her goodbye. I turned suddenly in the aisle and said, "Oh, by the way ... you didn't tell me your name. What's your name?"

"My name is Margery Jane Funk," she said. "Margie."

As I climbed down from the bus, I suddenly felt an added bounce in my step.

I smiled and, as I walked to a taxi stand, thought to myself, "I wonder if she makes vegetable soup."

I took a taxi to the seminary and walked around the building looking for signs of life, but there didn't appear to be anyone on the premises. Parked at the rear of the building was an old 1938 blue Chevy coupe with a red flashlight on top, like those on police vehicles. I called for anyone who might offer some assistance.

"Is anybody here?" I shouted.

In the distance, I heard a faint response. "Yes, I'm here ... I'll be right with you."

A young man came down and introduced himself. I explained my situation and he reminded me that it was a weekend, with no one in the office. He said I was welcome to spend the night on the extra bed in his room and then check in with the seminary office in the morning.

The man's name was Bob Smith and he and I would become roommates, and great friends throughout my stay in Seminary and for years thereafter. Bob was from Darien, Connecticut, and served as a preacher in a little church in Relay, Maryland. He worked as a volunteer fireman in the community, which explained the red flashing light on his car.

On those occasions when Bob had to be out of town, I gladly filled in and preached in his absence at the Relay church. While I'd preached a bit at Draper, the additional experience at Relay was very helpful and made me more comfortable sermonizing before congregations.

Sometime in mid-October, Bob needed to return to Darien to pick up some books at his family's home. I accompanied him to Darien in his Chevy. Bob had a quite extensive library of religion-themed books and retrieved selected volumes that might provide insights for future sermons.

On our return to Westminster, I said, "Hey Bob, let's stop by Johns Hopkins Hospital. I want you to meet someone I met recently." Margie and I had been corresponding by mail, and I was anxious to see her again in person.

My courtship of Margie was slowly advancing.

So, we stopped by the "Nursing Home," as the housing facility for student nurses was known. I called Margie from the main switchboard. She came running down the stairs and we were both elated to see one another.

We caught up on news since our previous meeting, and Margie introduced us to her good friend, Sandy Harvey, known as "Harve" to her friends.

Harve and Bob and Margie and I subsequently went out on a couple of double dates, to dinners and a movie. In time, Bob and Harve were spending a good deal of time together. The four of us became fast friends and made a great team together.

Harve was from Philadelphia. Her parents invited all of us

to visit for Thanksgiving weekend and treated us royally. We attended church together on Thanksgiving. The ride back to Baltimore in Bob's little Chevy coupe was a bit cramped, but we all laughed a lot and got to know one another well.

Shortly after Thanksgiving, Margie learned that a little six-year-old cousin had recently died. She wanted to be there for the funeral. Also, Margie's parents had recently moved to Johnstown, Pennsylvania from Somerset, so she was especially anxious to see them and visit their new home.

Bob suggested that I borrow his car for the trip to Pennsylvania. Because Marge wasn't precisely sure how to get there, we made a few detours along the way, but eventually made it to Johnstown, found their house and met her family. Over the next few days, I offered what support I could during that sad time and grew close to the family. Shared grief can bring people much closer.

By the time we arrived back in Baltimore, it was clear that Margie and I were girlfriend and boyfriend.

I had joined the Westminster choir, the "Seminary Singers." I was active in the choir when I was at Duke, and even on the USS Leedstown, the ship that took us to the Philippines, and was happy to get the chance to sing church music again at Westminster.

The Westminster Seminary fell under the jurisdiction of the Washington, D.C. conference, which was overseen by Bishop Oxham. The bishop was a tireless fundraiser for the Seminary and, on occasion, called on the choir to perform at events. The choir was conducting their annual Holiday concert in a Methodist church in Baltimore. Margie and Harve taxied out for the concert.

It proved to be a very busy first quarter in 1953. Very shortly after the Holidays, Margie's grandfather died, and again, we returned to Pennsylvania. Then, my friend Bob Smith fell ill with pneumonia and was sidelined from his seminary studies for the remainder of the semester. I served his church in Relay in his absence and the Church asked me to stay on as their interim minister. I agreed to do so.

My parents insisted that I save all my money, including all the money I saved from my paper route. I'd gone to Duke with four hundred dollars.

The father of a close friend from Duke was a minister who advised his son to keep a ledger of everything he earned and spent. Believing that a sound financial practice, I started keeping a ledger of my own. If I spent a dollar here and there, I entered it in my ledger.

By the end of the school year at Seminary, I'd been dating Marge for close to a year. I went through my ledger one night and tallied all the expenses I'd incurred on dinner dates and movies and such and found that the sum amounted to six hundred and seventy dollars.

"You know, Margie," I later teased her, "I've spent a small fortune for dinners and movies. I really think it's time for us to start thinking about getting married. I need to protect my investment!"

Shortly after that, Margie and I were both serving the church in Relay. We were clearly very much in love.

One night after spending an evening out, I gathered the courage, gazed deeply into those beautiful blue eyes and asked her to marry me. She said yes.

It was, then, and - after sixty-five years of marriage - is still my very best decision ever!

I rented an apartment two blocks from Johns Hopkins Hospital, and just a half block from the Nursing Home. There was, at the time, a prohibition against engaged or married women living in the women's housing dorm.

Margie visited the Dean of Nursing, and explained that

she wanted to get married, and that her fiancé was studying at Seminary with plans to be a minister. The Dean saw the wisdom in Margie's argument and let her continue living in the student nursing facility. She thus became the first engaged student to be permitted to remain at school. Margie broke the ice for women at Johns Hopkins.

One of our fellow seminary students performed our wedding in 1954 at the Relay Methodist Church.

I graduated from Westminster a year later, in 1956, and we started life's greatest adventure together.

18

FIRST MINISTRIES

While I was still in Seminary, I was serving temporarily as minister at Relay, Maryland, about eleven miles south of Baltimore. I substituted for Bob Smith at the church in Relay when he was sidelined with a case of pneumonia. While I eventually served larger churches as my career progressed, Relay has remained always among my very favorites. Because of the small size of its congregation, the bonds I formed with the congregants there were very strong, more intimate.

Relay also stood out in my memory as a particularly happy time in our lives. It was, after all, the first church that Marge and I served together after we were married.

When I first got the appointment, I'd drive down on Fridays after classes from Westminster and spend the weekend in Relay. The little Church was situated on the main line of the Baltimore and Ohio Railroad. Years earlier, Relay had been the stop where the line changed coaches. Locals could hear the trains changing engines and boxcars well into the night.

The main highway running north and south, I-95, was located quite near the church. Just off the highway was the Lord Calvert Distillery. On stifling summer days, in the absence of air conditioning, the church just opened the windows and let the breeze flow through.

What also flowed through was the strong aroma of Lord Calvert blended whiskey.

At the end of the fall semester, 1956, Bob returned to the area with a new Studebaker automobile his father had bought him. He was thus blessed with an embarrassment of riches, having two vehicles to his name. He asked me if I had any interest in the car. As it turned out, I did, and bought his Chevy coupe.

I've always considered that was one of the best trades I've ever made, a serviceable automobile for just one hundred and twenty-five dollars!

The congregation at the Relay church had just one hundred members. It had no parsonage at the time, so I needed to find a place to stay on the weekends. A married couple named Koerner lived across from the church and offered to rent me a room in their modest house. They were a lovely family, church members, hard-working, respectful, and very welcoming to me.

Mr. Koerner worked for the Baltimore and Ohio Railroad as a clerk in the main office. In his spare time, he worked as a printer. He had a press in his basement, where he produced fliers and brochures for small businesses in the area.

The couple charged me fours dollars a week for the room. It was in the attic of the house, where there were no separating walls, just rafters, a bare floor, and a cot. Nothing fancy, but the couple provided me with substantial country meals.

On my first Sunday evening there, Mrs. Koerner sweetly asked if I liked cucumbers. Wanting to please my host, I enthusiastically answered "yes, of course." When she served dinner, she laid down a huge bowl of sliced cucumbers on the table.

"My family doesn't care for them, so there's just for the two of us!" I looked at the huge bowl warily, but answered cheerfully, "How nice!" As things turned out, I should have tempered my enthusiasm. For the remainder of my stay there, dinner featured a steady diet of cucumber side dishes.

While I thoroughly enjoyed my stay with the Koerner family, I haven't eaten a single cucumber since.

A side benefit of my stay in Maryland was the chance to visit periodically with Shockley. For a time, he was stationed in the Port of Baltimore at the same time I was in seminary. He was serving as a Chief Petty Officer aboard the *Conecuh*, a former German vessel captured and re-commissioned during the War. I drove the forty miles south to Baltimore from Westminster and spent the occasional weekend aboard his ship. We sometimes took in a Baltimore Orioles baseball game at the newly built Memorial Stadium. When not visiting with Shockley, I was able to use his car to see Margie.

I completed my seminary studies in 1956 at Westminster. By that time, the Westminster Seminary had decided to relocate to Washington, D.C., and was re-named the Wesley Theological Seminary.

In my first official appointment after my ordination, I returned to the western North Carolina Conference. I served a "charge" that included four small churches near Pinnacle, located about a hundred miles northwest of my hometown of Carthage. Pinnacle then consisted of just a few stops, a post office, and a hardware store.

In the Methodist Church, a charge is a group of congregations that is served by a single minister and governed by a charge conference. Charges are different from "station" churches, which have a single minister dedicated to their church. The charge tradition began centuries ago when solitary preachers travelled between distant churches on horseback to serve the spiritual needs of geographically dispersed congregations. At the time, these itinerant preachers were called circuit riders. My Grandfather was a circuit rider.

The charge I was assigned included four churches in Stokes County. One was in King, just six miles southeast of Pinnacle; one was a little north of King; another was in Pinnacle, and the fourth just north of Pinnacle. Trinity United Methodist Church was five miles from Pinnacle.

Our stay in Pinnacle was most memorable for the birth of our oldest son on February 3, 1957, at the North Carolina Baptist Hospital in Winston-Salem. We named him Thornton Dixon Adams, Jr. and immediately started calling him "Tad," which has remained his nickname ever since.

All the churches in the charge had their own distinct personalities.

The appointment involved a good deal of travel. In addition to the regular services I held at the four small churches, I was doing a lot of driving to visit elderly shut-ins, nursing facilities and patients recuperating in hospitals in Charlotte and Winston-Salem. I had no travel expense budget to supplement my salary, and with all the driving, our family budget was stretched to its limit. Every year, I put about seventeen thousand miles on my little Chevy.

At an annual meeting of lay leaders, it was suggested that my salary be raised from eighteen hundred dollars to two thousand dollars a year. However, one senior leader loudly objected, insisting, "No preacher should make two thousand dollars a year!"

Having picked dewberries and labored in the tobacco fields as a boy, I was naturally quite familiar with work in agriculture. The Pinnacle area produced a good deal of tobacco. Farmers had to procure an allotment from the county agent to legally market the crop. The size of the tobacco allotment depended on the size of the farm. For instance, a one-hundred-acre farm might receive a six-acre allotment from the county to grow tobacco. The allotment system was intended to support the price of the state's most valuable agricultural resource, and to create a more equitable distribution of market share among North Carolina growers.

In the summer of 1956, the weather was especially severe, as storms wreaked massive damage throughout the area. A family in the King Church had a tobacco allotment but was simply unable to manage it that year, as a hailstorm had beaten down a good portion of its crop. Fearing that the whole crop might be lost, the family donated it to the church for the season. Farmers in the congregation banded together and raised the tobacco for the church, doing their best to salvage what they could.

I lent a hand. The work took me back to my boyhood jobs in the fields, "suckering" hornworms off the leaves and trimming unproductive leaves from the tobacco stalks.

Another of the churches in the Pinnacle charge raised sugar cane, which they refined into cane syrup and molasses. The farmers cut the cane stalks into manageable pieces and placed them on a grist mill. Then, with a mule harnessed to the millstone, they worked the mule in a continuous circle, grinding the cane stalks round and round, thus squeezing the sugar juice from the stalks. At that point, the women on the farm collected the cane juice and boiled it, reducing it into its end-products, syrup, and molasses.

One day, some members of the congregation invited me to participate in the process. I spent the entire day feeding stalks onto the mill. The work was repetitive and exhausting, but it certainly felt good to be contributing to the output of those farmers.

When we finished the day's work, the farmer who owned the cane operation offered me some praise for my work, saying, "Well, it's true what they say, Dixon: you can take the boy out of the country, but you can't take the country out of the boy."

On another occasion while in the Pinnacle charge, I was invited to visit a revival at a neighboring church in Pilot Mountain.

The revival movement began in earnest early in the eighteenth century, and really gathered momentum after the Civil War with an emphasis on social reform and personal salvation. Typically, a revival involved calling someone to come down to the altar from the audience. Unfortunately, at this revival, we couldn't find anyone willing to answer the altar call. So, I proceeded to tell the story of the night my Mother died.

The memory had lingered with me for years, and on the night of that revival so many years later, I emphasized the lessons I'd carried with me. Namely, that there are no guarantees in life; that we never know when we might see someone dear to us for the final time; and that we should take every opportunity to show our love.

After I mentioned that anecdote, a few people started trickling down to the altar, some with tears in their eyes. One woman became very emotional at hearing my story and fell into a near-collapse when nearing the altar. Many decades ago, that kind of heightened emotional reaction and physical convulsion was referred to as having a case of "the jerks." The woman's husband, who was a barber in Pilot Mountain, later related that she had long suffered from a nervous condition. While she was continually on the verge of a breakdown, she'd always stubbornly refused treatment.

Her response to hearing the story of my Mother finally convinced her to seek the help she badly needed.

Shortly after arriving in Stokes County, Marge and I needed to register to vote. Marge is from Pennsylvania. When she was growing up, most Catholics were registered Democrats, and most Protestants were registered Republicans. Marge's family were Republicans.

When I grew up in Carthage, eastern North Carolina was

entire town consisted of a gas station, a grocery store, a hardware store, the church, and a few houses. We'd spoken at church on several occasions.

The young man tentatively approached me and asked:

"Preacher Adams," he said, "I'm lookin' to get married. I was just wondering ... could you ... marry us today?"

"Well, sure," I said, "Do you have a lady to marry?"

"Yes sir," he said, "she's right over there," and he pointed to a pretty young woman standing in the door well of the store nearby.

"Well, you'll need a license. Do you have one?" I asked.

"Yes, sir, I do."

"Well, then, let's get in the car, we'll go and get you married."

We piled into my car, and I drove the couple to the parsonage. I needed two witnesses for the ceremony, so I telephoned a neighbor who lived nearby, and then recruited Marge as the second witness.

When the witnesses arrived and everything was in place, I performed the ceremony. When I finished the wedding service, I congratulated the beaming couple. I reflected briefly on the two ceremonies I'd officiated during the day: a funeral and a wedding. One, to celebrate a life well-lived and the transition from one life to the next; the other, to bless the wedded union of two people in love and focused on the road just ahead.

As I watched the couple sharing their moment, I glanced again at the marriage license and immediately spotted a problem.

"Oh, no," I said. "You got this license down in Winston-Salem."

"Yes, sir?" the groom said, quizzically.

"Well, that's in Forsyth County."

"So ...?"

"This is Stokes County," I said. "You can only get married with a license that's been issued in the same county."

The couple suddenly looked crestfallen.

After a moment, I said, "Wait a minute … I have an idea! Let's get back in my car."

The bride and groom and I got back in the old Chevy, and we drove five or six miles down the road until we were safely inside the Forsyth County line. By then, the bride was appearing frantic.

I stopped the car by the side of the road.

"Get out of the car," I said. We tumbled out of the car and walked over to the curb.

I looked back and forth at the hopeful couple, standing side-by-side on the curb, a slightly confused look in their eyes. With no further delay, I simply said solemnly, "I now pronounce you Man and Wife." The couple embraced again, now delighted to have advanced their status from "not-quite-married" to "fully-wed." At that, I instructed them, "Now let's get back in the car!"

With the vows completed, I drove the wedding party back to Pinnacle, and the handsome young couple walked off to a happy future together.

After serving the Pinnacle charge, I was next sent to Salem Methodist Church in Mount Airy, where I served from 1958 to 1960. When Marge finished her degree at Johns Hopkins, she took a job at Northern Regional Hospital in Mount Airy.

While serving in Mount Airy, we were blessed with the birth of our second son, whom we named Rodger Lee Adams. Rodger was born in the Northern Hospital of Surry County on May 27, 1960.

At Mount Airy, I took a six-week course at the North Carolina Baptist Hospital School of Pastoral Care, which was affiliated with Wake Forest University. There were around twenty of us in the course. We had classes from nine to ten-thirty each morning, and then turned to practical work ministering to patients. We were each assigned two ward rooms, with four patients in a room: another two rooms with two patients each, and two private rooms. We were, effectively, the Chaplains for any patients that occupied our rooms during that six-week period.

As part of our coursework, we were required to write detailed, verbatim reports describing any conversations we had with a patient or the family, whether in the room, the hallway, or the parking lot. The professor was a very strict grader, and my reports typically came back covered in red ink.

He continually hammered home the same message when evaluating my reports: "Where is the Grace?" He emphasized the need to always leave the patient with a feeling of solace or forgiveness or spiritual encouragement. In short ... with Grace.

A future minister later in my career would insist that parking lot visits didn't really count. In recent years, I've often kidded my fellow women church members after we've had a chat in the parking lot, "Now remember, Ladies, parking lot visits don't count!"

The Salem church was located just below the Blue Ridge Parkway. To get there, we had to drive up the narrow, twisting Black Snake Road past the Levering apple orchard. The daughter of an elderly church member had relayed an unusual request from her father. It seems the man had a passion for apples and always required a big bowl of them on the kitchen table. Marge and I would stop by the Levering orchard periodically to replenish his supply. We learned that if we picked apples directly from the trees, the cost was fifty cents a bushel. On the other hand, apples picked up from the ground were just twenty-five cents a bushel. Thus, we managed to find ourselves a bargain, while providing a steady supply for our fellow church member.

While at Mount Airy, Marge and I made good friends with a Moravian minister, Rev. Ray Troutman, and his wife. He had a church located a mile or so from Salem. Like Marge, his wife was from Pennsylvania, and we grew to be true friends. His Sunday service was always at ten in the morning, while mine was at eleven. When he was away, I'd preach for him and then drive back to my church and preach my own service. When I was out of town, we reversed roles. The friendship was mutually beneficial.

In 1961, we were once again on the move, this time sent to Lees Chapel, on the north side of Greensboro. I served there for five years, from 1961-1966. While in Greensboro, Marge worked at Cone Hospital, which was named after a major cotton manufacturer and industrialist in the area.

While serving at Lees Chapel, we celebrated the birth of our youngest son, Neil Smith Adams, on October 26, 1964, at Cone Hospital. Later, while Neil was attending the area's public schools, I served on the local PTA.

Around that time Greensboro was the site of a famous sit-in demonstration when African Americans were denied entry to the local Woolworth's. One day, a large group entered the store and sat down at the segregated counter of the store lunch fountain. When the men were denied service, they were arrested for disturbing the peace. The actions of the so-called "Greensboro Four" became a model for future peaceful Civil Rights demonstrations, as the movement gathered momentum in the activist 1960's.

In the late 1950's, Dad and Mumsy moved to Charlotte to be near her ailing sister. Over the next few years, Dad's own health declined steadily, and in November,1964, he died at seventy.

Dad had been my guiding light in the years following the early loss of my Mother. He was the foundation rock throughout my boyhood. He taught me much about life and work and was a faithful servant of his community and his church. For all of us children, he was the very model of decency.

Mumsy, whose kindness, financial acumen and business sense kept the family afloat during those perilous years of the Depression, would die in 1980.

In 1966, I was assigned to Grace Methodist Church in Kings Mountain. As Easter 1967 was approaching, the congregation eagerly awaited the annual Spring celebration of the most sacred period on the church calendar.

However, several minor issues had arisen that needed to be dealt with.

First, there was the matter of the ladies' knees. Normally, the choir was located directly behind the preacher in the pulpit and facing the congregation. These were the mid-1960's and dresses were getting shorter with the advent of mini-skirts. The knees of the choir members were increasingly visible to the congregation, a fact that had not gone unnoticed by some in the congregation.

On the morning of Holy Saturday, I visited the church and discovered the choir chairs had been moved. They now faced away from the congregation and toward the altar. The seats had very high seatbacks, so the women in the choir - and their offending knees - were now partially shielded from the congregation.

The second issue was of an acoustical nature. The organist was positioned to the right of me on the altar, quite near the pulpit. During recent services, the organist was playing so loud that the choir music was being drowned out altogether. The congregation couldn't hear a thing except the ear-splitting music of the organ. When I entered the church on Saturday, I heard a hammering sound emanating from the church. On closer inspection, I discovered the choirmaster at work inside the organ. She'd removed the back of the instrument and was nailing wooden blocks under the foot-pedals. The effect was intended to lower the volume of the organ.

On Easter Sunday morning, the organist played the organ beautifully. However, positioned just feet from me, I could witness her grimacing as she struggled to achieve the desired volume. The choir, the choirmaster and the congregation were all greatly relieved by the lowered volume of the organ.

But after the service, the organist approached me and implored, "Reverend Adams, you're going to have to call in a repair man. I just couldn't get any volume out of the instrument today." I assured her that I'd investigate the matter, but it was really all I could do to keep a straight face. Thus, ended the skirmish between the church organist and the choir master.

The final Easter emergency involved chewing gum. Many of our congregants were inveterate gum-chewers and would chomp away throughout the services. Then, - particularly, the younger gum enthusiasts - would apply wads of gum beneath the church pews. Over the years, the gum had made its way onto the hardwood floors of the church aisles and had created a terrible mess for the church.

A wealthy church member - Mr. De Brule, the owner of a large cotton mill - offered to fix the problem. He had the pews removed and professionally cleaned and the floors scraped, cleaned, and polished. The following Sunday, I made an impassioned plea to the gathered congregants from the pulpit begging them not to chew gum in church. I held a shoebox aloft showing the collected debris and gum-droppings as evidence of the miscreant gum-chewers.

"My parents would never let me chew gum in church!" I told the congregation in feigned outrage.

In 1968, Marge was offered a position in a local hospital for which she was very much overqualified, and subsequently found a job at a small hospital on the edge of Stokes County. The commute involved a 23-mile drive both ways at eleven o'clock at night, so it was quite a grind for her. But she would soon find herself in great demand.

Dr. Eugene Poston was the president of Gardner-Webb College, located in a little town called Boiling Springs, about nine miles west of Shelby. Marge was earning an excellent reputation in her field, and Dr. Poston recruited her to teach at

Gardner-Webb. While there, she met a nurse who had received a Master's degree at Emory University in Atlanta. Marge decided to apply to Emory herself and was duly accepted.

In 1968, we moved to Atlanta. The very first Sunday that we were there, we attended services at the North Decatur Methodist Church. My sons were talking with the minister's children, who mentioned that they were attending Bible class. Our boys asked if they could also attend the class. I chatted further with the minister and mentioned, in passing, that I'd worked on many youth programs while at Duke, High Point and some of my early ministries. The minister grew more animated and said he was looking for just such a person to take over the Youth Program at North Decatur. He offered me the post and I accepted. Meanwhile, Marge continued her nursing studies.

While I was developing the North Decatur youth program, I began a course of study at Emory and started working toward my own Masters in Christian Education.

I had yet another commitment in Atlanta, working at the Georgian Clinic, a facility for the treatment of alcoholism. The Clinic was housed in the Candler Mansion, the former home of the founder of the Coca-Cola Company. During my studies there it was eye-opening to see patients' gallant battle against this disease. No doubt, some suffered repeated relapses, and it was heartbreaking to witness their pain. But I witnessed the power of addiction, and it was truly joyful to see how many eventually triumphed.

It was, admittedly, a hectic time for Marge and me in Atlanta, but also enormously rewarding. We both were engaged in advanced learning while preparing for new paths in our respective careers.

While busy in Atlanta, we were, nonetheless, able to enjoy that great capital of the South. Our family had long been baseball fans. Uncle Raymond was a Philadelphia Phillies fan, while Dad was a follower of the Pittsburgh Pirates in the days before Major League Baseball expanded to the West and the South. Marge and the boys went to see Atlanta Braves games, when entrance to a game cost just a dollar. To this day, our boys remain loyal Braves fans.

After our graduations from Emory in 1969, we returned to Boiling Springs, where Marge resumed her teaching at Gardner-Webb and I served the little Sharon Methodist Church in Shelby, which dated back to 1851. We remained in Boiling Springs for three happy years.

Marge learned of a new teaching position opening at Lenore-Rhyne College in Hickory. Founded in 1891 and affiliated with the Lutheran Church, the school was expanding its nursing teaching program and Marge was interviewed for a position there. She accepted the position in Hickory.

Upon my return from my Atlanta sabbatical, I spoke with the District Superintendent and explained our evolving family situation. To keep the family close, I requested a transfer to the church in Hickory.

I was soon offered the post of associate minister and moved to First Methodist Church in Hickory in 1972.

19

HICKORY

In 1972, I was a newly arrived minister at the First Methodist Church of Hickory. At the time, I had an aging Buick that badly needed replacing. One day, I visited the local Oldsmobile outlet looking for a trade-in. I'd known the former owner as a member of the Hickory church and had written a letter of recommendation when he originally applied for the franchise. He had since passed away, and his son was now running the place.

I had my eyes set on a new Oldsmobile. The young man told me he'd let me have it at his cost. But I knew the game by that time. My job working in a service station just after returning from the War was a real education in car-buying. The dealer named a price of twenty-four thousand dollars.

I told the young man that I wanted to go home and consider it a while. I remembered that there was another Olds dealership miles away in Conover. I drove over one day and told him what I was looking for - the same Oldsmobile, same year, same model, with precisely the same equipment. He came out and told me I could have the identical car for four thousand dollars cheaper than the price my "friend" had quoted me.

I'd learned my lessons well from my days working in the service station and viewed the transaction as a promising start to my stay in Hickory.

New beginnings are always energizing, and I was anxious to get to work at Hickory. Initially, I worked with a minister named Charles Beaman. Charles had been a District Superintendent, was exceptional in his outreach programs, and showed great empathy for others. Together, we maintained an excellent working relationship. Charles visited hospitals on Monday, Wednesday, and Friday. I visited on Tuesday, Thursday, and Saturday. Charles preached on Sundays, while I continued to work with youth groups, driving the bus to a local beach outing or for a week at St. Simon Island, Georgia in the summer.

We began a very successful outreach program in 1976, a Sunday School class for young singles and married couples. We called the class "Pairs and Spares." The intent was to give young men and women a way to maintain a connection with the church after they'd left to go to college or begin a career path.

At first, the women of the Church registered mild objections to our use of the "Ladies Parlor" for the new program. They feared the younger group might disrupt their special area. In fact, the young people behaved admirably, and the program grew bit by bit, becoming one of the most popular groups in the church.

In another effort, we teamed with local ministers from Hickory and a few from outlying areas to form the Hickory Ministers Association. One of our outreach programs was an offshoot of an initiative by the local police department. While serving in Hickory in 1977, the local chief of police wanted to start a Chaplain's Program.

The Association ministers met every Monday morning to receive training in police matters and protocols. There were initially about fifteen of us involved in the program. Whoever was on call for the week received a two-way radio, a Chaplain's badge and remained alert in the event of an accident or death that might require a minister to assist an aggrieved family.

The program required a good deal of time and energy, and, over time, ministers gradually began to drop out. Within five years, there were just three of us active in the program.

Soon, we were on call every three weeks or so. It was a wonderful program, but, as the number of participants dwindled, the commitment was detracting from the time we needed for our own church responsibilities.

I was on duty one night in 1978 when I received a message indicating that the brother of a Hickory-area man had died in Baltimore. I was asked to locate the man and break the sad news to him. I found an address for the man, drove to his house, and knocked on the door. A woman answered the door and warily asked what I wanted.

"Hello, I'm looking for Mr. Evans," I explained.

Hesitating, the woman said, "Uhhh, ... he's not here just now?"

I pressed on. "Well, ma'am, would you know when he might be back?"

"No, I ain't got no idea." she said. "In fact, you know, come to think of it, we really don't even know who that is."

"Oh ... okay. I see. Well, thank you, anyway," I said, and turned to leave.

The woman again stuck her head out of the doorway and said, "Say, Reverend, what exactly did you wanna see him about?"

"Well ... I wanted to let him know that his brother in Baltimore has passed away."

"Ohhh ... is that so?" she said. "Well, I'll be darned ... Hey! ...

look 'ere, here the man is, after all. He's standin' just behind the door here!"

With that, the missing loved one magically re-appeared. His reticence in appearing at first was not my concern. I had a nice chat with him and offered my condolences on his brother's passing.

Charles and I believed that outreach programs kept the church close to the people, especially in those moments of need. We were both proud of our work, but Charles moved on to another assignment after just three years.

The next minister I worked with at Hickory was a kind man and a devoted minister but had encountered a host of personal difficulties while in his previous position. Tragedy seemed to stalk him.

One evening, his son was visiting a store, when someone entered the store with the intention to commit armed robbery. At one point, the situation turned violent. Shots were fired and the minister's young son was struck and killed.

The minister was understandably shattered by his son's death and remained hounded by the memory of what had happened for years afterward. Hard as he tried, he was unable to regain much peace of mind.

Over time, family turmoil began to take a terrible toll on his ministry and on his marriage. His wife arrived at a point where she could simply take no more. After a year or so at Hickory, overwrought and apparently unable to cope with her husband's fragile emotional state, she simply packed her bags one day and left without a word of explanation.

At the time, I was still serving as a police chaplain in the Hickory police department and was familiar with many agents in the region, both state and Federal. Local law enforcement initiated an investigation and tried to locate her, but she was apparently intent on keeping her whereabouts unknown. It remained a mystery where she'd gone.

The minister had done excellent work with the young people in the church, setting up recreational opportunities and services directed at their special needs. They, in turn, thought the world of him. But sadly, his days were numbered at Hickory.

By 1978, Marge was working as Director of Nursing at Catawba Valley Medical Center. An ophthalmologist in the Hospital was assembling a group to travel to Bolivia. Each year, he organized a trip to South America or Africa.

The group typically consisted of a ten-man construction team and a ten-person medical team. The construction crew worked on a renovation or re-building project in the chosen community. In this case, it was a church that needed an addition to the adjacent church-school. I was asked if I'd like to partici- pate as a member of the building team and eagerly accepted the opportunity.

Meanwhile, a medical team was gathered to perform cataract surgeries to treat a perennial plague so common in high-altitude countries.

We flew to Santa Cruz, where the church-school taught three student sessions a day. Catholics had classes in the morn- ing, Protestants in the afternoon, and adult education took place in the evening. The school was in desperate need of additional classrooms for five hundred students.

We built a new schoolhouse, one hundred feet-by-fifty feet. We started building on a Sunday afternoon. One of my jobs was to mix the mortar needed to install the footing. We then brought in bricks, and put the masons to work, some from our team, and some among the residents.

The medical team slept at a hospital in Monterey, convenient to their patients. Those of us on the building team just slept on cots near the school construction site.

Because there is relatively little rainfall in the area, the foun- dations didn't have to be built terribly deep. After the foundation was in place, the team put up wooden trusses and then a brick veneer. Soon we'd assembled everything but the roof. At the end of the two-week period, we dedicated the new schoolhouse.

Being part of that project was a gratifying experience. The medical team had addressed a pressing therapeutic need, while the construction team filled a gap in the local educational efforts.

It was especially rewarding to see how the dynamics changed between the native people and the Americans over the course of the project. At first, Bolivians kept to themselves, while our team worked solely among our fellow Americans. But about half-way through that first week, the two sides were intermingling, conversing amiably, and working very efficiently with one another.

The trip proved to be fine example of how people from widely different backgrounds can work toward a common goal. I was very blessed to have had that opportunity. On that occasion, my building work served as my ministry.

One night in 1978, I was at a meeting with a friend, Frank Parker, who was a local realtor, a participant in our Bible class and a member of the Masonic lodge. At dinner later, we discussed a mutual minister friend who had recently suffered a tragic accident. The man was trimming a tree in his yard, when, perched high on a ladder, he slipped and fell to the ground. The fall killed him.

The loss of a beloved local pastor was a blow to the entire Western North Carolina Conference, where the minister was held in high esteem. The family's misfortune was made worse by the fact that they were eventually required to vacate the church parsonage to make way for the incoming minister. While Frank and I commiserated over the terrible loss and its impact on the man's poor family, I started thinking aloud about my own family's situation.

"You know, Frank," I said, "I shudder to think what would become of Marge and the boys if something were to happen to me. I really need to give more thought to the family's future security."

"Dixon," he said, "What you really need to do is to buy the family a house of their own."

"Frank, you're absolutely right," I said. "Why don't you start looking at houses for me."

My broker began hunting for houses and, in short order, found a home that filled the bill. Sadly, the previous owner had been struck and killed in an automobile accident, and the woman's son wanted to sell the place as quickly as possible.

By then, Marge had left Gardner-Webb and had some savings accumulated from her work there. With that as a down payment, we were able to get a mortgage that ran to three hundred and fifteen dollars a month. Within just three days or so, we found someone to rent the place for three hundred and twenty-five dollars a month.

My broker friend Frank accepted a ten-dollar monthly fee in exchange for managing the rental property.

20

BREAD MINISTRY

During my tenure at Hickory, I'd known many uplifting moments, as well as some genuinely challenging ones. By 1980, after an eight-year stay there, I was feeling the need for a change … that it was time to re-charge my batteries. I decided to take a sabbatical.

I discussed the idea with Marge, and she was very supportive. However, we were both quite mindful that we still had a family to provide for.

One day, I ran into a friend from church, Joe Garner, who sang in the church choir and was a member of our bridge club. We talked about my upcoming plans. He was a sales representative for Prudential Insurance in the Charlotte area. He listened to my plans and came up with a novel idea. He suggested that I join him for a period at Prudential as his assistant. The job would certainly provide me the change of pace I craved while I pondered the next chapter in my life. It would also provide a steady income during my sabbatical.

After completing the training required by the North Carolina Insurance Commission to gain state certification, I began working at Prudential in early 1981, commuting to Morganton, about a half-hour drive up Route 40 from Hickory. I quickly learned the basics of the insurance business. My role generally involved maintaining customer accounts, monitoring billing, and collecting premium payments. The job was far removed from my ministerial duties, and I appreciated the fresh outlook and new perspective. However, over time, I found that diversion and a reliable income were simply not enough. I began to feel the pull of my ministry vocation tugging at me once again.

I'd worked at Prudential for about two years, when, on Christmas Eve 1982, I received a call from the bishop. We were on very good terms after my time in Hickory and had formed a close friendship in the years since. The bishop extended his blessing to Marge and me and wished us the Season's greetings.

He added one more item. He informed me that the minister at Moore's Chapel had, sadly, contracted advanced Alzheimer's and was no longer able to maintain his pastoral duties. The bishop asked me if I'd be interested in taking over the assignment in Charlotte. After I discussed the matter with Marge, we agreed that I was more than ready to return to the pulpit.

Moore's Chapel United Methodist Church was built in 1871, and named after a generous benefactor, Gabriel Moore, a successful businessman in the area. His bequest provided land to seven churches and, initially, the charge included all seven congregations. Over the years, the charge was re-aligned to just two churches at the time of my appointment in 1982.

My sabbatical had left me feeling fully renewed and prepared to resume my ministry.

On the Sunday after Christmas, I reported to Charlotte and began a very fulfilling two years at Moore's Chapel. Marge had a satisfying job as Director of Nursing at Catawba Memorial

Hospital, with increased responsibilities that called on the full range of skills she had gained over decades as a nursing professional and teacher. Happily, we had a relatively manageable commute between Hickory and Charlotte on weekends.

Conveniently, the people who were renting our house in West Hickory had recently found a house of their own to buy, so we were able to move back into our house at virtually the same time they moved out. Once again, the Lord had moved in mysterious ways.

Most importantly, Marge and I felt that we were in a place we were meant to be.

While I was settling in at Moore's Chapel, Marge was living in Hickory. All three of our boys were then away at school, so we were, at least temporarily, "empty nesters." One day, a doctor's wife at the Catawba Hospital dropped by Marge's office and gave her a quart jar of bread starter, specifically, sourdough starter.

Marge brought the starter home and showed it to me. While grateful for the thoughtful gift, she didn't really know what to make of it. She exclaimed emphatically, "Dixon, I simply don't have time for this!" I looked at the material on the jar and said, "Good gracious! I don't have time for it either," and set it temporarily aside.

Later that night, after we'd had dinner, read the paper, and watched the news, I picked up the jar again and examined the package more thoroughly. I discovered that the bread-making process is much more elaborate than I ever imagined. Suddenly, I became more intrigued and decided to look further into the idea.

"Good grief," I said to Marge the next morning, "I read the directions last night. This isn't something one does in a single sitting. It's much more involved. You feed the starter into the dough, let it sit eight hours or so, then you combine it with flour and knead the dough. Then you let it sit out for a day."

I decided that I might just try my hand at bread-making, and soon became fixated on the mixing, the chemical reaction of yeast and flour, the kneading. I came to understand that bread cannot be rushed. Dough needs time to breath, to mature. Like all things, bread needs time to develop into something truly worthwhile.

I was pleasantly surprised by my initial efforts, and with that, a whole new chapter of my life had begun.

After the weekend, I took the bread starter with me back down to Charlotte and began to do some additional research on the art of bread-making. Marge came down to spend the Christmas weekend together. I had just made three loaves of bread, my inaugural attempt as a bread-maker. To my delight, it was well-received.

Marge suggested that I take over a loaf of bread to a friend of ours, Miss Alton, who was a shut-in. She was thrilled to get a fresh loaf of warm bread. Next, Marge remembered another friend, Miss Mitchell. Her response was the same. There was something organic in the giving of bread that elicited such a warm reaction.

And that is how my Bread Ministry began.

Within days, the word of our "bread visits" had quickly spread throughout the Moore's Chapel congregation. It soon became a staple part of my ministry to include freshly made bread with my visitations.

A while later, I read in a local Shelby paper about a woman, Pearlie Allison, who made "prayer rolls." She delivered rolls to friends and people who were somehow troubled or otherwise bereft. That seemed like a splendid idea to me.

Soon after, I learned of a woman in our church who had given birth to a baby with cyanosis, what was then sometimes referred to as "blue baby syndrome." The condition described a change in skin tone due to a chronically low level of oxygen in a baby's blood. I visited the woman and delivered the rolls and she appeared very moved by the gesture. From that point, I started making prayer rolls for other afflicted persons, delivered with my prayers for their recovery.

In time, I started to experiment with other varieties of bread. A friend, Les Morrow, was a former police officer from Claremont, not far from Hickory. After retiring from his Highway Patrol position, he was elected a City Councilman in Claremont.

Les always had a keen appetite for pepper jack cheese. After visiting a cheese factory up in West Jefferson one day, he brought me back a pound of the cheese.

I enjoyed it very much and thought that I might try it as a bread flavoring. It, too, was very well received. Soon, I was looking into other baking opportunities. I made cinnamon raisin bread, and Hot Cross buns, which I'd long associated as a staple around the Easter season. The tradition of eating Hot Cross Buns on Good Friday dated back many centuries and remains to this day a commemoration of the death and Resurrection of Christ.

When I came to the Church in Conover, I continued my bread-baking and expanded my distribution. Since I retired from the church, I have no church members to visit, so I just jokingly refer to them as … "my customers." To this day, I find sustenance and solace in bread-making. As Jesus said, "I am the bread of life: he that comes to me shall never hunger; and he that believes in me shall never thirst."

By then, my old friend, Harold Hipps, was living in Nashville, Tennessee, and serving as a national board member of the Methodist Church. After he and I both retired, we'd get together on occasion in Nashville and visit the Grand Ole Opry, and such. I took him some bread one time and he thought it was "out of this world," in his words.

Later, I wanted to mail some bread to him, and that started a bit of an adventure.

I was finding it difficult to find boxes that were suitable for shipping bread loaves.

One day, I was visiting my son Tad, who was then a pharmacist in a local hospital. I spotted a box left over from one of his shipments that appeared to be the ideal size for my purposes. He was only too willing to let me use those boxes.

I addressed the box to my friend, used a Magic Marker to blacken the Baxter Labs name on the box, and sent it along to Harold.

When it arrived in Nashville, the postal authorities apparently found the box worthy of further inspection and set it aside for special handling. Later, two postal inspectors visited Harold's house and waited on his porch for him to return. When he arrived, they insisted that they needed to make sure there was no contraband enclosed in the parcel. They opened the box in his presence and found … a loaf of pepper jack cheese bread.

In the wake of that comical episode, Harold sent me a book about making bread, entitled "The Spirituality of Bread."

I discovered that the history of bread-making is as old as that of humanity itself. Ancient texts discuss the critical role of grain harvests and distribution in ancient Rome. Bread guilds were considered sacrosanct among the skilled trades of the day. It took as long as seven years for a young apprentice to attain the status as a master bread-maker.

The Christian tradition is filled with allusions to bread-making. It is believed that at the Last Supper, Jesus urged His disciples to share His bread, His Body in celebration of His gift of everlasting life. Christ likened the breaking of bread among fellow believers - the slaking of physical hunger and thirst - to the spiritual sustenance provided by His Body, His Blood, His Word.

In retirement, I began a series of speaking engagements with church groups in the area. I was asked by a women's group in Newton to put together a program speaking to the women about the bread making process and its deeper significance over the millennia. I delivered a few more lectures, and then started teaching classes in bread making, thus spreading the "bread ministry" beyond my solitary efforts.

A local funeral director established a support group that offered comfort to spouses who had recently lost loved ones. They initially met at a small local restaurant. In time, the group outgrew that space, as people came in from surrounding churches in Conover.

I was asked to add some spiritual guidance as part of my lectures. I also drew on my magic show background and the combination added a bit of lightness and solace.

And, of course, there was the bread itself. Initially, I was making three dozen rolls for each meeting. Over time, the need swelled to six dozen ... and continued growing further. In time, it became simply too difficult for me to meet the growing demand alone. Fortunately, the bread ministry has expanded to include more bread makers, who have since been able to fill the need.

My personal bread count over forty-three years has been impressive. I started keeping an official record-keeping in 2001: 16,539 loaves of bread; 1,547 dozen prayer rolls.

That first quart of bread starter led to an entirely new form of ministry for me. It continues to this day, thanks to the work of many volunteers who have followed in our footsteps and the loaves that have been baked and distributed over the years have grown commensurately. I eventually combined my various bread-starters into one linked mix, with origins in Egypt, the Holy Land, the Red Sea, Saudi Arabia, San Francisco, the Yukon, and the Oregon Trail.

At last, ... one unified, ecumenical bread starter.

Over the years, I made three trips to England on pastoral matters, the first on a Methodist Heritage tour in 1978, visiting sites relevant to the development of Methodism. The second was a visit with a study group run by a professor from the University of North Carolina Charlotte.

In the early 1980's, I had another opportunity to visit England on a heritage tour. As a Methodist, I was most interested in viewing the many historical sites that were instrumental in early Methodism. We were able to visit the birthplace of John Wesley, and the places where he preached. It was an awe-inspiring experience to climb into the pulpit and stand in the very steps where Wesley preached. For this Methodist minister, it was a very moving and inspirational experience.

On that latest trip, I took a brief course at the University of London. The theme of the program was "Living the Ancient Gospel of Jesus Christ in Today's World." The seminar was taught by Rev. Dr. Birtwistle, a leading British theologian of the day.

Dr. Birtwistle's work made a lasting impression on me. During his presentation, he made some observations that crystalized my thinking on preaching and influenced my future ministry.

The gist of his thesis was this: If you study and memorize and preach the words of the Old Testament, and live by those words alone, you will be a Good Jew. And if you study the letters of Paul in the New Testament and preach those words and live by them, you will be a Good Paulinian.

If you study and follow the teachings of Revelation, he continued, you will be a Good Revelationist.

He then warmed to his subject. If you want to live by the teachings of Jesus Christ, you need to study the Gospels of Matthew, Mark, Luke, and John, particularly, the fifth, sixth and seventh chapters of Matthew ... the Sermon on the Mount.

Then he delivered his simple, elegant summation. If you really want it all in a nutshell, here it is: Simply love God with your heart and soul, and your neighbors as yourself, and treat them as you'd have them treat you.

Those words, echoing the words of Scripture and so simply stated by Dr. Birtwistle, have formed the core of my preaching ever since that lecture in London forty years ago. When I boarded the plane in London to return to North Carolina, I left increasingly focused on my mission and with a renewed sense of purpose.

And I was anxious to resume my Bread Ministry. During the long flight, I had plenty of time for thought and reflected once again on my newly discovered passion. Just what was it, I wondered, that was so satisfying about the experience of baking bread? Was it the physical feel of kneading the dough into just the right texture? The wondrous aroma of yeast and dough as it rises to a crusty, brown perfection? The simple satisfaction of giving sustenance to others? Or just the final incomparable taste of fresh, warm bread spread with butter or jam?

It was probably a little bit of everything. But I couldn't wait to return home and share those joys with others.

21

THE PARSON AT PLAY

In balancing a lifetime of study, work, and pastoral care, I've also made time for diversions that have given our whole family great enjoyment over the years.

From the time I was a boy, I was interested in magic and found delight in performing feats of illusion. The reaction was especially thrilling when coming from children, who have a unique capacity for wonder and surprise.

While I was working with youth groups, I started taking an increased interest in magic tricks. Initially, I learned to perform some illusions to entertain the children around campfires and such. One of their perennial favorites was the aforementioned trick of "sawing" one of the children in half. A sure-fire hit!

I also tried out some magic tricks when I was a student at Duke. As a freshman, I was in downtown Durham one day and was waiting for the bus back to campus. It was bitterly cold, so

I walked into the Washington Duke Hotel to keep warm while I waited.

Inside the lobby, there was a cigar stand, and I spotted a man behind the counter who was performing some magic tricks. He had a half-dollar, and an empty bottle of Coca-Cola, both covered by a handkerchief. Then, with a flourish, he removed the hand-kerchief and suddenly the half-dollar appeared inside the bottle.

In another illusion, he approached someone smoking, and asked for his cigarette. He pressed it into a handkerchief with his thumb, flipped the handkerchief and suddenly the cigarette had disappeared. I was impressed by the man's dexterous display and approached him. "Say, how did you get that half-dollar into the Coke bottle?" I asked.

"Well," he said, "for twenty-five cents, I'll show you the secret."

I gave him the change and he handed me a little box that he said contained the secret to the trick. My bus had just arrived, so I hurried aboard and sat down just before the bus pulled away. I opened the box, glanced at the paper, and realized that I'd been taken.

Suddenly, it occurred to me that the man's most impressive trick was to make my twenty-five cents disappear!

After the bus rolled back onto campus, I was still feeling a bit embarrassed. I returned to my dorm and ran into some friends who lived across the hall from me. I noticed that all of them were smoking.

"Aww, no," I said to one in mock disgust, "you shouldn't be smoking! That'll be the death of you. Say, Bill, do you have a handkerchief?"

My friend looked puzzled but handed me his handkerchief.

"Now, let me borrow that nasty cigarette of yours."

My friend obliged, and to his surprise, I pulled the same disappearing act with the cigarette that I'd seen performed earlier at the Washington Duke Hotel. In pulling off that trick, I felt that I'd partially redeemed myself as an amateur magician. I've maintained an avid interest in "magic tricks" ever since.

Over the years, I expanded my repertoire of illusions. I sent away to a company called Percy Abbott's Magic Shop in Ohio where, for forty dollars, I received a book of tricks with complete instructions. The tricks seemed to delight the children in my youth ministries.

In coming years, after I'd become a minister, I performed "magic shows" at hospitals, for groups of seniors, church congregants, high schools, summer camps, and retirement communities in the area. Word started to spread, and soon I was, much to my surprise, in high demand. At one point, I had to restrict my appearances locally, lest my act grow stale and become overly familiar to audiences.

After I retired, I revived my performances, visiting area hospitals. Patients would be wheeled into the shows in wheelchairs and beds. Some elderly patients might be dozing, but standing behind them were nurses and staff, who often appreciated the shows as much as their patients.

Shortly after my maternal Grandfather died, my Grandmother gave me his beautiful pocket watch, which I treasured then and still do. She was living with her sister who was also widowed.

One day I visited them and showed them a few tricks I'd learned. They got a big kick out of them. Grandmother exclaimed, "Dixon, your Uncle Ed was also a talented magician. He travelled up north and performed magic shows from school to school throughout Ohio, Michigan and Indiana."

She told me that he had a trunk filled with his illusions that, to my amazement, was still upstairs. She gave me the trunk and, suddenly, my repertoire of tricks had grown even larger. The keepsake from my Uncle has been precious to me for years, but

I was equally thrilled to learn that my interest in the art was a long-followed family legacy.

Even after I stopped doing the formal magic shows, I found that I could do spontaneous tricks for people when the occasion called for some levity. One evening, Marge and I were in a crowded restaurant and were told that the wait for a table would be forty minutes. A little girl stood nearby waiting with her family. I walked over to her, winked at her parents, and said to her:

"Let me see your wrist for a minute, young lady."

The little girl shyly held out her hand. Her mom and dad smiled as they anticipated her growing excitement.

I pulled my handkerchief from my breast pocket and wrapped it around her wrist in a square knot, nice and secure.

"Now make sure you hold on to that handkerchief tightly," I said. "Make sure that knot is really secure."

She did just that. Her expression turned to one of fierce determination to hold on tight. I waited a second or two for dramatic effect, and in an instant, pulled the knot loose. The handkerchief slipped through her little hands and back into my pocket.

Her blue eyes opened wide. "Where did it go!" she shrieked, sporting a look of wonder as the scarf disappeared before her very eyes.

Bringing a smile to the faces of children and seniors over the years was one of the great joys of my life. I've now been a member of the International Brotherhood of Magicians for more than fifty years. I certainly did get my forty dollars' worth of entertainment from old Percy Abbott's.

When I was a little boy, I was fascinated by clowns. My Dad took me to the Circus whenever it visited on tours of the South. After I had a family of my own, I took my sons Tad, Rodger, and Neil to see the shows. Going to the Circus became a rite of passage for the family.

I was asked to dinner one night by a leading couple in the

Charlotte church. The husband mentioned that he was a member of the Scottish rite of the Masonic order. I told him that my Dad had been a Mason for fifty years, and that I'd followed in his footsteps since 1949. (In fact, in 2019, I received a plaque in recognition of my having been a Mason for seventy years.)

The conversation shifted to the Shriners, a fraternal organization that had entertained as clowns in parades and charity functions for many years. The Shriners were founded in the 1870s by a group of Masons in New York. Shriners were, in their founding years, mainly known for their devotion to fun and frivolity. By the 1920's, however, the group had increasingly focused on charitable works. In the years since, Shriners have raised many millions of dollars for the construction of hospitals for critically ill children

"You know," I said, "that's something I've always wanted to do, but just never got around to it."

The dinner ended, and a few days later, I received a surprise visit from two members of the Oasis Shriners of North Carolina. They arrived dressed in their clown costumes. The next thing I knew, I was a member of the Oasis Shriner clowns.

In 1984, I decided to attend Clown School in Virginia for a two-week course. There were about fifty of us in the class. The course was taught by "Buttons the Clown" and "Frosty Little," who, for many years, were two of the acknowledged stars of the Ringling Brothers Circus.

In my clown act, I dressed the part of a hobo, named "Parson the Clown." I wore a tuxedo that I'd found in a local Goodwill thrift shop, for which I paid four dollars. While certainly affordable, my tuxedo looked a bit too new. It still had its original price tag on it! A friend suggested that it needed "a more lived-in appearance," and thought he had the ideal solution. We took the tuxedo and hung it on his laundry line. Then my friend got his shotgun out of his garage and fired several rounds of buckshot at it. In no time, the outfit had the tattered and torn appearance of one having spent many years riding the rails.

The Clown School instructors taught us how to apply the make-up that is essential to the trade. It was a real art to master the subtleties of creating just the right exaggerated facial expressions: happy, sad, silly, surprised. When marching in parades, some of the clowns drove in the tiny red cars that are a staple of the Shriner parade tradition. I typically walked along the perimeter of the route, nearest to the crowds, engaging in cheerful banter with the people.

I carried balloons with me that were tied to a stick and handed them to children as I passed by. The balloon sticks were covered by a wider plastic straw. When I handed the balloons to onlookers, they would naturally grab the straw handle. Before they knew it, the loose-fitting balloon stick would rise out of their grasp. The children got a huge kick out of it.

Among the little things I learned from my instructors was some grooming advice. I'd grown a beard and a mustache while on an earlier building mission in Bolivia. I was told that I would need to shave my mustache if I was serious about becoming a clown. It turns out that no self-respecting clown would ever sport a mustache.

Every year, I preferred to attend the Grand Finale performance of the Circus, getting the full picture of all that went into the Ringling Brothers production. It was an enormously complicated operation. I was especially interested in the way the clowns helped shepherd the movements of the animals during the performance. Clowns weren't just there to make funny faces!

Over the years, I participated in many parades staged by the Shriners as part of their charitable efforts.

When I was a student, I loved to participate in amateur theater. As a member of the Dramatic Club in high school, I appeared in several theater offerings. Although the plays were often quite frivolous, we had a lot of fun. When I wasn't rehearsing for a role, I often helped in building stage sets. My Grandfather had been a carpenter. He worked for many years on housing developments within the Pinehurst golf resort. Granddad built cabinets and woodwork, doors, and furniture for the Pinehurst developments. From watching him closely at work as a boy, I picked up many carpentry skills that made me a quick study at building stage sets.

After I left the army, while working for Bell Telephone in 1949, I had a chance to resume my work with a local theater group in my spare time. I had some good friends at Greensboro College, an all-women's school, who were part of the College Dramatic Society at Greensboro. They had to import boys from outside to take the male roles, so after I got off work at four-thirty, I'd go to the college and participate in rehearsals.

There was an initiation process to make the three of us official members of the College Players. We were told to meet at the switchboard in the dorm at six in the morning. Our initiation challenge was to convince the skeptical guards that three young men had a legitimate need to gain entrance to a girls' dorm in the wee hours of the morning. Happily, we spun a yarn that convinced the guards to grant us admission to the girls' quarters.

The plays were not especially memorable, but they were wholesome fun for all, and I thoroughly enjoyed the experience, just as I had in high school.

I had roles in two or three plays. One production, I recall, was titled, "They Did Away with Uncle." In it, I played the minor role of a British detective investigating a murder. As such, I was required to put on an accent. I did manage a few words in a British accent, albeit one heavily influenced with the cadence of the Carolina Piedmont.

On seasonal occasions, I played Santa Claus during the Holidays. A church group was having a dinner to celebrate the

Season but didn't have any entertainment planned. Marge suggested that I take on the role of Santa for the evening.

I paged through the Sears Roebuck catalogue and found a Santa costume that looked the part. Having stuffed my suit with a pillow to add the necessary heft, I added the obligatory black belt, floppy red cap and flowing white beard. I handed out little gifts and treats to children while "Ho-Ho-Ho-ing" my way through the evening.

Thereafter, whenever we spotted a store Santa, my son Tad would invariably say, "Dad, he's not the *real* Santa Clause. He's just a helper. We know who the *real* Santa is!"

Looking back, I realize that my most truly enjoyable moments - those that brought me the most joy - were those that Marge and I shared with Neil, Rodger, and Tad.

In 1989, while we were serving our church in Conover, I rented a house in Garden City, South Carolina with four of my fishing friends. Initially, we just rented the house for a weekend. It cost the entire group ninety dollars. The owner later informed us that we could have rented it for the whole week for just one hundred and ten dollars.

We decided to make the trip an annual affair and extended our visit through the entire week. So, the next year, we rented the same house for the week, this time in October, when the intense summer heat had dissipated, and the fish were beginning their annual migration southward. In the meantime, a few more fishermen friends said they wanted to join us.

Sadly, Hurricane Hugo had taken dead aim on Garden City a month earlier, destroying forty percent of the area's houses, including the house we'd reserved. We were forced to locate another property.

In time, some golfers wanted to join the annual trip, and we had to rent a second house to accommodate the growing crowd. The trip was informally designated "Fishers and Golfers." Later, another friend asked to join the fun, but made it known that he wanted nothing to do with fishing or golfing. He just wanted to loaf for the week. At that point, the group became known as "Fishers, Golfer and Loafers."

We told jokes, teased participants about their respective angling and golfing skills, and shared stories of how some of our fellow preachers have fared. My role eventually became that of baker and bread-maker after a heart condition meant casting for striped bass was no longer possible. While the number of participants has decreased in recent years, we've continued our annual trips and remain dedicated fishers, golfers ... and loafers!

22

TO CONOVER ... AND RETIREMENT

Not long after my appointment at Moore's Chapel, one of the church's lay leaders approached me and asked me for some advice.

For years, the lay leadership had lobbied to have Moore's Chapel recognized as a station (one church). As things stood for years, the church was recognized as a charge, administered by a "charge conference" dealing with the administrative matters and overseen by a District Superintendent.

"We've been promised for years now that we would one day go station," he said, "but we keep getting the same response. 'Well, I really don't think that's going to be quite possible this year,' we're told, year after year after year."

Time and again, the lay Church leaders took the matter to the District Superintendent, and repeatedly, the mattered was deferred.

The lay leaders were, quite understandably, very discouraged. I mentioned a possible strategy that might improve their prospects.

"Why don't you write a sincere, respectful letter on your own, directly to the bishop and tell him how strongly you feel about the matter," I suggested. "But please ... please, don't mention my name."

The lay leaders followed my suggestion, and a week later, I received a call from the bishop who agreed that it would, indeed, be an opportune time for Moore's Chapel to become a station church. The District Superintendent followed up with a call of his own and echoed the bishop's remark. The lay leaders were overjoyed and thanked me for my advice.

I had been serving at Moore's Chapel for nearly two years, when the bishop called again, with still more news.

"Brother Adams," he said, "I've been giving serious thought to moving you to another church. The position in Conover is going to be available pretty soon." Then he added earnestly, "Now, this is just between you and me. Pease don't mention this to anyone." I gave him my word that I'd keep quiet.

Historically, the Conover appointment had not been an especially coveted one.

A few years before when we were living in Shelby. I was working at a small parish near Gardner-Webb College, a Christian liberal arts school in Boiling Springs, which was a predominantly Baptist community. The small Methodist church there had just thirty members.

I remember chatting one day with a colleague from a larger Methodist church in the Shelby area. It had been suggested to him that he might be selected to assume the Conover appointment.

"Oh, noo-oo", he insisted. "I'm looking for a much larger church than Conover." He was clearly quite ambitious and had his sights set on a prestigious appointment that might advance his career. In fact, he did eventually become a District Superintendent.

Nonetheless, several ministers were openly eyeing the Conover post for themselves. Even as some were confidently talking to me about their prospects, I had to keep my lips sealed about the bishop's having already been promised me the position.

After the appointments were announced in June 1984 and it was revealed that I was, indeed, going to Conover, my friends and colleagues teased me for keeping the appointment a secret. That created some awkward conversations.

"I'm your best friend," one joked to me, "and you didn't even tell me!"

"Well," I said, "I was asked by the bishop to keep my mouth shut ... and that's exactly what I did!"

While we were still living in West Hickory, my realtor friend, Frank Parker, who had found our Hickory property, suggested that I should consider buying some property in Rock Barn. A large parcel of land had been purchased by a developer who'd made a fortune in the nursing home business. He now had plans to build a golf course - called the Rock Barn Club of Golf - with new homes built nearby on the property. My realtor considered it a promising investment for our family.

At first, I put the matter off, explaining that we were content with our current living situation, and I didn't really have any need for access to a golf course. After all, Conover was just six miles from Hickory.

However, soon after beginning my assignment in Conover, I had to adjust my thinking.

As it turned out, the Conover church no longer had a parsonage. The previous minister from Conover had a grown son and daughter who'd both moved back in with them. The minister's own house only had one bedroom. He spoke with the church officials, who decided to sell the parsonage, and let the minister buy a house to accommodate his recently expanded family.

As a result, my earliest days at Conover were marked by endless commuting: six miles in the morning to work, then back to Hickory for lunch, then back to Conover for the afternoon, then back home in the evening. After just a week of that routine, it was clear that the situation simply wasn't going to work.

I touched base, once again, with Frank Parker, who started looking for a house nearer Conover. In short order, he found a place in the Rock Barn area, located right on the golf course. The home was laid out on one level, which was ideal for us. Living there would entail much less climbing upstairs than we'd encountered in the Hickory house. So, we took the plunge and established a comfortable residence at Rock Barn.

One group I started in Conover focused on the senior citizens in the congregation. The group was called "The Good Timers" and created social opportunities for that often-neglected segment. At an early discussion, one participant suggested a vote to elect officers for the new group.

At that, a chorus of disapproval rose from the other members: "No! No! No!" was the general consensus. "No officers, no organization, no meetings! We just want to get together once a week! Meet! And eat! And have fun!" The group has been extremely successful.

In 1984, while in Conover, I met a young man named Gerald Lofton. I was serving as the leader of a local Boy Scout troop and, with retirement in the not-too-distant future, was on the lookout for a future leader to take over the reins. I had first recruited Gerald years earlier as a substitute for me as Santa Claus at a children's Holiday party.

Next, I introduced him to clowning with the Shriners and finally to a role with scouting. Most people don't realize the commitment required to be an effective leader in scouting, and many choose to leave after just a year or two. Over the years, Gerald has been exceptional and an excellent role model for young men. He's carved out a remarkable legacy over the years, ushering seventy-one scouts to Eagle Scout status.

Harold Thornburgh was a long-time leader in the Conover congregation, and a prime example of how friendship in the church can last through multiple generations. Harold's son Jeff followed in his father's footsteps as a church leader. The three of us often vacationed together, as Harold and Jeff were long-time participants in our annual fall fishing trips.

Jeff's young son, Lee, tagged along with his father and grand-father. Lee liked to play with his miniature race cars, and the two of us would play make-believe NASCAR games together, topped off by a treat of Klondike Bars. Remarkably, that little boy graduated from high school in 2020.

On my ninetieth birthday in 2016, I received a kind note from Harold, thanking me for "the impact you've had on our family, especially our Lee … and the influence you've had on this young man … for that Jeff and I are so grateful."

Those memories are so very precious.

We saw a good deal of growth in the Conover church in the years I served there, and under subsequent ministers. The Bishop and I became the best of friends. Even after his retirement, we maintained a collegial relationship.

I stayed in Conover for eight years. The boys were now grown and all three were successful in their chosen careers: Tad in pharmacy, Rodger as a technology consultant, and Neil, as a chef in Catawba. Marge was enjoying success in her administrative career in nursing. Now it was time for me, too, to look for fresh vistas and new challenges.

And so, in 1992, with my eyes looking forward, not backwards, I announced my retirement.

While eagerly anticipating retirement, I quickly learned that there was still much work to do.

In August 1992, Hurricane Andrew hit Homestead in south Florida. The storm was rated a Category Five force. A quarter of a million people were left homeless in Dade County alone, battered by winds reaching one hundred sixty-five miles an hour. Our new young minister was instrumental in putting together a rebuilding team of volunteers from the western North Carolina conference.

Our group travelled down to Florida and spent two weeks there. The devastation was just remarkable, as many homes were destroyed entirely. We helped rebuild wherever possible. The 1990's proved to be an extremely active period for hurricanes, and we returned to Florida in subsequent years to participate with rebuilding teams.

After we had had completed our work in Homestead, several of us went on a side-trip to Key West and took in the sights. I complimented the tour guide on his excellent job, and he asked me if I ever visited Boston. I informed him that I had family who lived in the area. He urged me to just mention his name the next time I visited New England. Sure enough, shortly thereafter, I went to Boston to visit Shockley and Frances, and we received free transportation around the city throughout our stay.

One day in 1996, Tom DeLucas, the chairman of the Catawba Republican Party, confided to Marge that Senator Bob Dole of Kansas was going to travel to Catawba County to give a speech. The Senator was then the Republican nominee for President. Perhaps assuming that I was also a Republican, Tom asked Marge if I might be available to give the invocation before Dole's speech.

She said she'd ask me. I said, "Sure, I'd be happy to."

When the day of the GOP meeting arrived, I gave the invocation prayer and sat at the head table, right next to Senator Dole's wife, Libby. We chatted amiably and enjoyed a pleasant lunch.

After the speech, I was approached by another Methodist preacher with whom I'd preached years before at a revival. After the meeting had adjourned, he looked around and remarked furtively, "Well, Dixon, it looks like you and I are the only two Republican preachers in Catawba County."

"Well, speak for yourself, Ray," I said.

"Whaddaya mean?" he said. "You're not a Republican?" he exclaimed.

"No, Ray, I'm a Democrat. Always have been. Registered in Stokes County in 1956," I said.

"Then, Dixon ... what the hell are you doin' praying for us Republicans?"

"Well, Ray," I explained, "they asked me, and I would never refuse a request for prayer." Pausing, I added, "Not even for a Republican!"

In 1994, the Flint River in Georgia incurred massive flooding, as Tropical Storm Alberto carved a swath through southwestern Georgia. Our re-building team from North Carolina went to Georgia to lend assistance. The river crested at forty-three feet, taking many lives, and causing damage that took many months to rebuild. Our team rebuilt quite a few homes that had been damaged in the deluge.

In the wake of the storm, we travelled to Albany, another town hard-hit by the floods. Albany is located quite near Plains, Georgia, the home of former President Jimmy Carter. One Sunday, we visited the little Baptist church in Plains, where Mr. Carter was teaching a Sunday school class.

He didn't have prepared remarks, nor did he speak from the pulpit, but simply stood in the main aisle of the church. He spoke of his experiences and tied them to reflections about Scripture. After the Benediction was said, he stayed and greeted all in attendance as we exited the church.

At one point, I visited the men's room very briefly, and

couldn't help but notice how squeaky clean everything was. I remarked at that fact to one of the women who was a church usher. She told me that on Saturday mornings, the President's wife Rosalyn Carter could be seen carefully cleaning the restrooms, while the former President was busy outside mowing the grass.

Again, in March 1997, flash floods swept through Falmouth, Kentucky, near Cincinnati. The Licking River overran its banks as ten inches of rain fell, requiring the evacuation of the entire town. That was my last experience with our local rescue teams, but the group remains active to this day in responding to natural disasters and emergencies throughout the region.

In 2011, Clarence Pugh, a friend of mine who headed the Rotary Club of Hickory, was assembling a group to visit the World War Two Memorial in Washington, D.C., and asked me if I'd like to come, as they had some extra spaces to fill.

I jumped at the chance. My friend Clarence drove us to Asheville, where we stayed a night in a hotel, before driving to Spartanburg, South Carolina for a morning flight to Washington. We received the royal treatment at every step along the way. The Asheville police provided an escort to the South Carolina line, and finally, a Highway Patrol escort accompanied us to the Spartanburg Airport.

When our plane landed in Washington, the organizers had brightly colored water hoses saluting the plane. Yet another police escort led us to the Memorial. There we were greeted by Senator Bob Dole who had spent a good deal of time working on Veteran's issues, both in Congress and in the years after his retirement. The Senator waited by the door to welcome all the North Carolina veterans as we exited the bus. Once again, Libby accompanied him. I chatted with her briefly and we had a good laugh about our previous meeting in North Carolina when I offered the prayerful invocation from a Democrat on a gathering of fervent Republicans.

Libby confided to me, "You know, Dixon, just between you and me, I used to be a North Carolina Democrat, myself."

Shortly after I returned from the Philippines in 1946, an old Army buddy visited me in Carthage. He suggested that I come visit his family's home in Pennsylvania. Sometime later, I travelled up to Pennsylvania, where we toured the Pennsylvania Dutch country. The area was stunning amid the brilliant fall foliage. I was especially attracted by the appearance of HEX signs everywhere. With their unique configurations and colorful designs, they added a unique flair throughout the local landscape. I thought they were very creative and coveted one of my own.

In 2003, Marge and I returned to Pennsylvania for a family funeral. We found lodging for the visit at an Inn that bordered the field where, on September 11, 2001, terrorist attacks crashed a plane in Somerset County, Pennsylvania.

While in the area, Marge and I visited antique stores and, along the way, I spotted a HEX sign that really caught my eye. I bought it, took it back to Conover, and gave it a place of honor on the front of our house.

Not long after erecting the sign, we started to hear that our purely decorative sign was becoming the subject of some odd speculation. Some neighbors wondered if we had become devil worshippers! Marge insisted that I remove the sign to quiet the concerns of the neighbors. I complied with her request, but must admit, occasionally, I still get the urge to put the sign back up.

Time and time again over the years, I've been reminded of the far-flung friendships of my brother Shockley. It seemed that, even in our retirement, the sun never set on Eldon Shockley Adams, Jr.

Marge was a Board Member of the North Carolina Psychology Board, and, in 1993, attended a regional conference in Mobile, Alabama. While she was busy with meetings and various business agenda, I set off to look at some local sights. There were only a few parts of the old naval installation that were open to the public, but I climbed aboard the USS *Alabama*, on which Shockley had served during the War as a boiler tender. The ship was permanently moored in Mobile.

I was chatting with an older volunteer guide who was showing people around the ship. In passing, I happened to mention that my brother had served on the ship during World War Two.

"Really," he said. "What was his name?"

"Eldon Shockley Adams, Jr." I answered.

"Whaaat? ... Saaam? ... You're Sam's brother??" he said, growing more animated.

He then proceeded to give me a grand tour of the ship, showing me the boiler room where Shockley worked and regaling me with stories about Shockley from many decades earlier.

"This was Sam's work-space." "This was Sam's bunk." All this, nearly fifty years after the War.

On another occasion we were up in Boston, visiting Frances sometime after Shockley had died in 2001. I stopped at a naval base and was touring the USS *Constitution* with my son. We stopped at a hot dog stand to grab a quick lunch, and I told the attendant that my brother had served in the Navy during the War. I mentioned Shockley's name.

"Awww, Sam? Heck, I know old Sam!" he said. Suddenly, I felt like I was standing once again in the glow of Shockley's friendship.

"Hey," the attendant said warmly, "What can I get ya, my friend? Have anything you want."

A few years later, the golf course developer at Rock Barn announced his plans to host a professional golf tournament. Certainly, having an event like that would add prestige for the club, and likely add significant value to the property. Thus, in 2003, the PGA Champions Tour arrived for the inaugural "Greater Hickory Classic at Rock Barn."

At the 2014 event, I was working as a volunteer driver for the week of the tournament, chauffeuring players between the Charlotte airport and the golf club. I'd drop the player off, and give him the keys to the new Cadillac, which was his to use for the remainder of the tournament.

On the morning of the pre-tournament opening ceremonies, I dropped off a player who'd just flown in from South Africa. I handed him the keys and rushed off to watch the ceremonies, as they were going to include an air show featuring five Black Hawk helicopters demonstrating their maneuvers. The air show was already underway when I arrived.

I walked over to the area where the ceremonies were being held in hopes of getting a better view. Unfortunately, the crowds were enormous, and I couldn't get anywhere near the roped-off area. I decided to walk back home, just a few doors down the road from the clubhouse, in the hope that I could still get a glimpse of the aerial performance from our house.

As part of the show, one Black Hawk was meant to peel off from the group formation and swoop straight down over the crowd. Instead, the aircraft came in at an altogether different angle and sped directly over my head as I walked along the sidewalk toward our house. The chopper's powerful updraft lifted me entirely off my feet and spun me about in mid-air, a bit like Dorothy in the "Wizard of Oz."

I landed with a thud, my head hitting the curb, somewhat the worse for wear. An ambulance was shortly on the scene and took me to the local hospital. When I awoke there, my son and his wife were laughing at the sight of me. While I survived the incident, I was still somewhat disoriented, and badly battered and bruised. In fact, I still have a blood blister on my lip as a souvenir of my encounter with the Black Hawk helicopter.

To this day, friends remind me of the day I took my unscheduled flight.

23

BEES IN THE BELFRY

On a brilliant Sunday morning when I was just a boy, my family was waiting outside the beautiful Carthage United Methodist Church for services to begin. As usual on these days, we listened patiently as the older men told stories and shared their experiences. My Granddad, who was a carpenter by trade, noticed that, on the side of the church near the roof, a swarm of bees was continually entering and exiting a hole just under the roofline.

Granddad, Dad, and Uncle Raymond decided that they would try to fix the wall. A few days later, they arrived with tools in hand, and, over the next few hours, removed an entire side of the weatherboarding from the affected area, and erected a new siding. In the process, they managed to salvage a good portion of honey from the comb in the roof.

For some reason, the men in our family had a good deal of experience handling bees. Dad had his own beehives in our back yard. He seemed to have a sixth sense of how to handle a swarm, and, unlike many who tended to shy away from contact with bees, he had a respect for the critical role that bees played in farm culture.

Bees pollinate crops from vegetables, nuts, apples, berries, pumpkins, and flowering plants. Without bees, we humans would go hungry, and the world would be much less beautiful.

Dad taught me not to fear them but instructed me in the proper way to approach a swarm. He even passed along a bit of ancient lore. Dad told me to beat on a tub to prevent the bees from swarming and keep them near the hive. This practice was thought to have originated in England centuries ago. As it turned out, the tub-thumping was meant to warn neighboring farmers that one was not trespassing on his land, but merely following a swarm of bees.

On one occasion, a local townsperson reported a swarm in a nearby wooded area and asked for some help. Dad, Granddad and Raymond approached the swarm. I was left to stand on the edge of the woods, when I heard a strange sound that frightened me a bit. I described the sound to my Dad, and he reassured me that I had just heard a harmless whippoorwill.

When I was working at the church in Hickory in the 1970's, my oldest son Tad was studying an ant farm he'd received as a Christmas present. He was fascinated by the way the ants worked together. They each appeared to have their own assigned roles in the ant colony. Tad had always been interested in nature, and I was happy to encourage his interests. He asked me if we could acquire some bees so that he could study that species, as well.

I thought it was a good idea and went into the barn loft in Carthage. Years earlier, Uncle Raymond and I had built a sixty-by-thirty-foot garage, with one bay for the car and another dedicated to storage. I climbed into the loft and found some old beehives that Dad had used many years before. I brought the hives back to Hickory. Next, I looked in the Sears Roebuck catalog - where else? - and found that Sears did indeed sell bees. Sears was the Amazon of its day.

I ordered the bees and very shortly they were delivered to the post office. Upon their arrival, I received a rather insistent call from the local Postmaster: "Dixon, you come down here and get these bees outta here!" he bellowed. "They're startin' to buzz around the post office and they're making me awful nervous."

The package of bees was ingeniously constructed for its time. The packaging was wooden, roughly a foot and a half long, and eight inches wide, with protective screen wire on each narrow side. Inside the core of the package was a box containing the Queen. A little container of sugar water was included to nourish the bees while they were in transit. There would always be a few bees that weren't quite confined within the box. The stray bees hovered close to the package during their journey, as the nervous postmaster had discovered.

Around the same time that we started Tad's bee project, I was playing handball one day at the gym and fell after returning a shot. My fall resulted in a broken foot. It was January, with ample snow and ice on the ground, so I was pretty much restricted to the indoors for five or six weeks. Tad gave me a book titled, "The ABCs and XYZs of Bee-Keeping," which I read cover-to-cover during my convalescence.

During my confinement, I combined my newly acquired knowledge of bees with what Dad and Granddad had taught me. I managed to construct a hive in which Tad could closely observe the peculiar behavior of bees.

I discovered that beekeeping was more common than I'd known. Through inquiries within the community, I learned that here were six local people that kept bees. Together with my fellow bee-fanciers, I started the Greater Hickory Beekeepers Association. We held our meetings in the conference room of a local savings and loan.

As word spread of our apian activities, we started hearing from more people with the same interest, some in the country on the outskirts of town. Finally, I was asked to teach a course in beekeeping at the local community college. Ultimately, we maintained three hives in the back yard of the parsonage, just adjacent to the church.

On one occasion, I was asked to preach at a revival in a little country church. I arrived early, and on this beautiful spring evening, I was chatting with a church member. I had a Volkswagen square-back, a little station wagon, at the time. The man noticed that I had a beehive in the back of my car. Soon, the subject turned to bees. He mentioned that, at present, he had a swarm that was living on his property quite near his house. My interest was piqued.

"There's a bee swarm right now that's landed on my fence post," he said.

"Say, would you mind if I took a look at it?" I asked.

"Yeah, go ahead and look at 'em. Frankly, you can do whatever you want to with 'em. I sure don't want 'em." he said.

With that, I grabbed a single hive from my Volkswagen, and we walked the short distance to his house.

When we arrived at his house, I immediately saw that the swarm had formed. It resembled a bag of bees hanging on the fence post. I took the beehive and strategically positioned it just below the swarm. I then stepped to the side of the fence post and gave it a good, swift kick. Just then, the entire swarm fell on top of the hive, which had a beeswax foundation.

By then, it was time for me to return to the church to preach at the revival. When the service was over, we returned to the man's house to find that all the bees had disappeared into their new living quarters. I put a lid on the hive and took it back home. The resident of the house was happy to have seen the last of his visitors, and I was happy to have added a fourth bee colony to the parsonage's back yard.

News of the incident spread around Hickory and soon I was receiving calls from people all over town who needed help dealing with unwanted clusters of bees.

One day, I was in downtown Hickory for a meeting. As I was nearing the office for my appointment, I noticed, in the distance, people scurrying about, anxious to avoid a swarm of bees.

A man confidently waved passers-by along their way. "No need for anyone to worry," he assured onlookers. "We've called a beekeeper. He'll be here shortly to take care of the situation."

In time, the professional beekeeper did finally arrive. He wore a veil, protective headgear, and haz-mat clothing from head-to-toe, generally looking like a Martian invader.

He went to work but was clearly struggling and didn't appear to be making much headway with the bees. He voiced increasing frustration with his efforts.

I approached the beekeeper and quietly suggested, "Excuse me, young man, could you indulge me for a moment?" I pointed to a particular spot on a branch of the tree. "Would you just saw off this branch, right here," I said.

The young man was dubious but did as I asked and sawed the branch free.

I was dressed in my street clothes with no protective gear except a baseball cap. I reached for the limb and calmly carried it over to the hive the beekeeper brought with him. I shook the limb, and the bees began to descend into the hive.

The crisis had subsided, but I was later called on to intervene in subsequent bee removals on quite a few occasions.

One day, Tad said he wondered if it might be possible to examine the bee behavior more closely. He asked me if we could have a hive installed inside the house!

I considered the engineering required and agreed to give it a try. I bought a small hive at the hardware store, with a single frame and glass panels on both sides. There was an entry portal on the outer side with tubing that ran through a wooden block and then under the window, allowing the bees easy egress in and out of the hive.

We positioned the hive in a window in our den, where Tad was able to monitor the bees closely. Our friends just loved it and it proved to be a great conversation piece. Soon, all the members of the Beekeepers Association started building beehives with glass sides so that people could get a close-up view of the hives.

Overnight, our family household had grown a bit larger. Marge. Dixon. The Boys. The Bees.

When Tad went off to state college, he was hoping to find a course in beekeeping. To his disappointment, there was no such course available in North Carolina. But he did find a course in a satellite program at the University of Ohio in Wooster. The teacher was Dr. Thieu. As he was giving Tad a tour of the school, Dr. Thieu introduced us to a young woman who assisted him in the program.

"She's from Winston-Salem," he added. At the end of the semester, we were returning for the Holidays, when Tad announced that he would be stopping along the way in Winston-Salem.

"What do you need to stop there for?" I asked.

"One of my classmates lives there and needs a ride home."

It turned out that Tad's classmate was the girl that we'd met that night on the tour, and they'd started seeing one another.

A year later, they were married.

I'd long ago heard that honey has exceptional therapeutic properties. When we were boys, Shockley used honey to nurse our little dog back to health.

Soon, I was about to witness its miraculous healing powers up close.

A local neighbor and church member, Bennie Giles, suffered terribly from chronic allergies. I already had hives set up in the back yard and gave her a quart of poplar honey from local poplar trees around the house.

Poplar honey is produced by bees that gather nectar from tulip poplar trees. It is darker in color and has a stronger taste than lighter spring honey. It has long been thought to ease muscle and joint aches. My friend started dosing with a bit of the honey and found that her allergy problems were greatly relieved.

Bennie owned a beautiful little Boston Terrier, a female who was her constant companion and the joy of her life. The dog was about to give birth to a litter of puppies. When the puppies were born, the firstborn of the litter showed virtually no signs of life.

The veterinarian put her aside and remarked, "I don't think this poor little thing is going to make it." He continued to deliver the rest of the litter.

After the rest of the puppies had been delivered, Bennie started to leave. She then turned and insisted on taking the failing puppy home with her, unwilling to leave her to die alone on the vet's table. She stayed up through the night and did everything she could to coax the dog to life, even using an eye dropper with medicine and sugar water to try to nourish her.

Nothing seemed to work.

Finally, she looked over and saw the jar of honey that I'd given her that had helped relieve her allergies. As a last resort, she reached over, dipped a finger into the honey and rubbed it on the puppy's lips. In just seconds, the puppy started to smack her lips, weakly at first, and then with increasing gusto. Over the next few days, she regained full strength.

Days later, Bennie brought the dog over to our house. She said, "Dixon, I just knew this little girl was destined to be yours." We next needed to give her a name and settled on the obvious choice. We called her "Honey." When we registered her with the American Kennel Club, her official name was "Lady Honey Field."

In no time, she became a treasured member of the family. She was always there, eagerly waiting for me when I came home from a day's work. She lived to the ripe age of sixteen. She was, indeed, a honey!

24

REFLECTIONS

"God Moves in a Mysterious Way."

I've heard that verse from the William Cowper hymn throughout my life and am truly convinced that it is true. On many occasions, I've come face-to-face with that reality.

I have a very good friend named Ronald Williams. Ron has a genuine zest for life, and a succinct way of getting his point across. Whenever he wants to emphasize an observation he's made, or his agreement with someone else's, he'll add the exclamation point: "And, that's for dang sure!"

Ron lives about a block from us, and every morning around five, arrives at my house and drives me to the fitness center at the Catawba Memorial Hospital. There, we get in our forty-minute workout. I've always been an early riser. Even today, I get up at 3 AM, then nap until a bit before five, when Ron arrives. We start our workout around 5:30. After our exercise regimen at the fitness center, we have coffee in the break room until about seven, chat with the rest of our friends, and catch up on the latest news.

These morning workouts provide excellent exercise, a time to relax with good friends like Ron and others, and moments for leisurely reflection. I've found it worthwhile to reflect on the blessings, the people, and the remarkable things that life has brought my way.

In 1972, while I was at the First United Methodist of Hickory, I met a wonderful woman, Grace Whitlock, who served then as a church hostess. People like the Whitlocks are the bedrock of a congregation: constant, reliable churchgoers who faithfully serve the community, and remain just as steadfast in their private friendships.

Grace died recently at the age of ninety-eight. For years, she kidded with me about being my senior. She jokingly warned me that, despite my relative youth, I must never forget to respect my elders. We shared a warm sense of humor and had a lovely friendship.

I've been the Whitlock family's minister for decades, having officiated at the weddings of her three beautiful daughters and her son and grandson. I performed Christenings for their children and grandchildren, of which there have been many. Most recently, I preached at Grace's funeral.

On the occasion of a grandson's Christening, she informed me that she had already prepared the holy water.

"What on earth do you mean, Grace?" I wondered.

"Well, Dixon, I did just as you suggested. I put the water on the stove, turned up the heat ... and just boiled the hell out it!"

My long friendship with the Whitlocks - and with countless other families - has encompassed virtually everything about the ministry that I've treasured over the years. Together, we've shared celebrations of life's joyous moments and supported one another through the more difficult times. While seeking to serve others' spiritual needs, I've found myself enriched as well.

Naturally, there have been occasions when I've found myself in uncharted waters, but those have often been among the most rewarding.

In 1970, I was serving at the tiny Sharon Methodist Church in Boiling Springs. My son Rodger came to me one day and said he wanted a home-made tie. Ties of the 1970-era were typically wide, featuring paisley designs and wild patterns of rainbows, geometric shapes, and vibrant colors. I gathered a variety of diverse fabrics and created a tie that I thought Rodger might like. He loved it. His warm response encouraged me to make more ties and expand that portion of his wardrobe.

After my Mother died in 1934, Dad became the family tailor. He had a sewing machine of his own for many years, but unlike the newer electric models, Dad's was driven by a foot-pedal. If I had trousers that needed shortening or a tear in my jeans that needed darning, Dad would do the mending. I learned quite a lot about the art of tailoring just by watching him.

One Saturday, I officiated at a wedding at the Sharon church and, at the post-ceremony reception in the hut behind the church, chatted briefly with Mrs. Prine, whose husband was a representative of Singer Sewing Machines. They had been touring the country together giving marketing demonstrations of Singer's latest products.

I mentioned that I'd recently made a tie for my son. Mrs. Prine said she was starting a sewing class on the following Monday and that I was welcome to join them. I was intrigued by the idea and decided to attend the initial class, expecting that I might learn some pointers that might improve my tie-making skills. When I arrived, I discovered that I was the only man in the class. Nineteen women ... and me.

Making me even more uneasy was the fact that the first sewing project the class undertook was to make ... a dress. I felt like a fish out of water but proceeded gamely. All the women had tape measures and busied themselves taking each other's mea-surements. Needless to say, I did not participate in that portion of the class, but discreetly observed the women from a distance.

When I got home, I asked Marge if I could have her measure-ments for the dress. Over the weeks of the class, the women very graciously helped me and answered my awkward questions. In time, I got the hang of things and felt more confident about my efforts.

Marge was teaching nursing at Gardner-Webb College in Boiling Springs at the time and had a formal affair coming up. The College had recently announced the appointment of its new President and had planned a ball to commemorate his inaugu-ration. Marge suggested that I make a gown for her to wear at the formal dinner.

A few days later, I went to a fabric store and bought the ma-terial for Marge's gown. I subsequently went to Sears and bought a sewing machine of my own and started sewing. My creation turned out to be a formal, floor-length dress in light blue. (Later, I altered the dress, cutting it to knee-length for office and casual wear.) As the Christmas Holidays were nearing, I made Marge yet another dress for an annual Holiday party for the Gastonia District ministers and their wives.

Marge and I went to the President's Ball and had a wonderful time. Marge wore the dress that I made for her in the women's sewing class and looked just lovely. She was, yet again, the pretti-est girl in the room. And - in my admittedly biased opinion - the best dressed one, too!

That marked the end of my brief career as a fashion designer. I gave my sewing machine to a woman who worked with the Play School program, who put it to good use creating dolls and toys for the children.

After I retired in 1992, the District Superintendent requested a favor of me. He asked me to tend to a charge of three African

American churches in the area: St. Paul's in Newton, Mount Beulah in Sherrills Ford, and Providence Church in Catawba. I was happy to oblige him. The appointments were in a fairly tight circle, affording me the opportunity to continue ministering, and gave me enough free time to start an enjoyable and productive retirement. I'd preach on Sundays at Providence at ten am, at Saint Paul's at eleven am, and then preach every other Sunday at Mount Beulah. The appointment lasted just two years, so it wasn't a huge commitment in time. Best of all, I met some truly remarkable people along the way.

In 1993, an African American woman congregant approached me one Sunday after services at St. Paul's in Newton. Like other women in the congregation, Church was a major emphasis in her life. She was dressed in her finest for the occasion, wearing a crisp white dress, and a striking broad-brimmed hat. She asked somewhat timidly if she might speak with me privately about something that had been on her mind for quite some time. "You won't mind if I'm frank, will you, Reverend?"

"No, my dear, feel free to say whatever's on your mind." I said.

"And you're sure that you won't be upset with me?"

"Goodness, no. Speak your mind," I assured her.

"Well, Reverend Dixon, we've been friends for a while now, and you know I think the world of you." She seemed fidgety, avoiding eye contact, obviously a bit nervous about how to proceed.

"It's just that ... I've noticed that... with passing time, you seem to, ... well, Reverend,"

"What is it, dear? Please ... do speak up!" I insisted.

"Well, Reverend, it may just be my imagination," she said, now smiling, "... but you seem to get Blacker every Sunday!"

At that, I broke into convulsive laughter, and it took me a while to compose myself.

"I hope I haven't spoken out of turn, Reverend," the woman said.

"Not at all, dear," I answered. "Actually, that may very well be the nicest thing anyone's ever said to me!"

I realize now that all the events of my life - even the occasional detours - have eventually led me to something worthwhile.

As I wrote earlier, I enjoyed an extraordinary friendship with Mrs. Florence Dockery Jones, my neighbor on McReynolds Street in Carthage. But her husband was always something of a puzzle to me. What I knew of him was simply a recollection of stories I'd heard from my family or from local town lore. In portrait, he was a proud son of the Confederacy, who had served his region. After his wartime imprisonment, he returned to a remarkable career as a local industrialist, became one of the wealthiest men in Carthage, was a respected civic leader and held a lay leadership position in the First United Methodist Church of Carthage. While I knew only the thumbnail sketch of the man, I was certainly impressed by what I'd heard.

But sometimes there are odd twists in life that disclose a fuller picture. Such was the case with William T. Jones.

About ten years ago, the people of Carthage had a legend confirmed that had only been whispered about before. A local Carthage woman had purchased the old Jones Mansion and converted it into a bed-and-breakfast. During her renovation work, she grew very interested in the Jones story, and became a relentless researcher into the great man's history.

After exhaustive searching, she learned a startling fact about Jones: William was, in fact, born the son of a slave mother and a white plantation owner. As a boy, he was eventually freed by his father and became a carriage painter. The rest of his amazing career unfolded like a legend.

Now, my family has had strong roots in Carthage for more than two centuries. I had grown up in Carthage and spent a good deal of my early life there. And, as a boy, I'd been one of Mrs. Jones's closest little friends and confidants. Yet, until a decade ago, I never had an inkling about her husband's full story. William T. Jones was, in fact, a Black man.

As a boy in the segregated South of the 1930's, I'd seen stores where Blacks were not even permitted to enter. They waited outside, verbally gave their orders at the door, and waited for their purchases to be brought to them.

Now, after a lifetime, we'd finally learned the liberating truth about this luminary of our town. Like many of Carthage's long-time townspeople, I was overwhelmed by a mixture of pride and humility at this eye-opening revelation.

William T. Jones was a Black man. Hallelujah, Lord! Hallelujah!

There was an old saying in our family when I was growing up: "The gifts most often recollected are the ones the least expected."

I've noticed, over time, that life has been continually handing me gifts, even when I may not have immediately recognized them as such.

But they've been there all along, a continuing string of gifts: providence, … serendipity, … miracles, large and small. I've had my momentary setbacks, as we all do, but I've been amazed how life has enriched me with life-affirming moments … and each of those wrapped in faith and love.

My beautiful children – Tad, Rodger, and Neil.

Our evening dinners with Neil, and the joy of chatting about his and my workdays. The memory of installing Tad's beehive into the house and new roommates … "the boys and the bees." My seeming uncanny knack for jinxing the office whenever I visited Rodger at work. All those precious little moments.

An endless roster of faithful friends. A rewarding life in the ministry.

And above all, meeting the love of my life on a Greyhound Bus.

It's all so clear, now. Faith is the guidepost to a truly blessed life. Love is its ultimate reward.

Yes, love - both given and received - is the most astonishing gift of all. Of that you can be certain.

And that, my friends? ... *that is for dang sure!*

APPENDIX 1

DIXON'S MINISTERIAL APPOINTMENTS

- Draper: First – 1953
- Relay, Maryland: (Baltimore Conference) – 1954-1956
- Pinnacle Circuit: – 1956-1957
- Salem: Mount Airy – 1958-1960
- Lees Chapel: Greensboro 1961-1966
- Grace: Kings Mountain – 1966-1968
- Sharon - Boiling Springs: Shelby – 1969-1972
- First: Hickory (Associate): – 1972-1980
- Moore's Chapel – Steeleberry: Charlotte - 1982
- Moore's Chapel – Charlotte: 1983-1984
- First: Conover – 1984-1992
- Retired – 1992
- Newton Circuit: – 1993

APPENDIX 2

RECIPES FROM THE BREAD MINISTRY

Sourdough Starter

INGREDIENTS

- 1 package dry yeast (1 tablespoon)
- 1/2 cup lukewarm water (105 degrees)
- 2 tablespoons sugar
- 2 cups warm water (105 degrees)
- 2 and 1/2 tablespoons all-purpose flour

DIRECTIONS

Mix yeast with 1/2 cup warm water.

Mix sugar with 2 cups warm water and flour.

Add the yeast mixture. Put in a glass jar and cover with cheese cloth or clean cloth and allow to sit for five days at room temperature. It should be foamy and have a yeasty aroma. Put this mixture in refrigerator for 3-to-5 days.

Take out of refrigerator and feed with the following:

- 1 cup warm water
- 3 tablespoons potato flakes
- 1/2 to 3/4 cup sugar, depending on how sweet you want the bread

Mix well and feed the starter. Leave out on the counter for 8 to 10 hours. Remove 1 cup to make bread and put back in refrigerator for 3-to-5 days and feed again

Sourdough Bread

In a large bowl, make a stiff batter of the following:

- 1 and 1/2 cups warm water
- 3 Tablespoons sugar
- 1 teaspoon salt
- 1 cup Starter
- 1/2 cup cooking oil (Canola)
- 6 cups bread flour (Pillsbury)

Mix with dough hooks or by hand — knead until you have firm dough. Grease another bowl — put dough into bowl and turn over until top of dough is greased. Grease wax paper and cover bowl. Let stand all day and overnight. (Do not refrigerate.) Punch dough down and place on floured surface— then knead 8-to-10 times. Divide into three equal parts and place into greased loaf pans. Cover with greased wax paper. Let rise 4 or 5 hours (all day is OK.) Bake in 350-degree oven until brown and sounds hollow when thumped. Time depends on your oven — 20 to 35 minutes.

Grain Bread

Follow the same directions for Sourdough Bread but use just 5 cups of bread flour and 1 cup of grain flour (Roman Meal Original Cereal), plus 3 Tablespoons of wheat germ (Kretschmar). Makes 3 loaves.

Cinnamon Raisin Bread

Follow the same directions for Sourdough Bread but add 3 teaspoons of cinnamon to the flour and 1 and 1/2 cups of raisins to liquid ingredients. Makes 3 loaves.

Cheese Bread

Follow the same directions for Sourdough Bread but add 1 and 1/2 cups of grated sharp cheese (Pepper Jack) to the dough. Makes 3 loaves

When in A Hurry ... (Half the time)

When time is short and you need to speed up the process, use yeast. Simply add 2 teaspoons yeast to your warm water and 2 teaspoons of sugar, and let it work for a few minutes.

Stir until smooth.

The Parson's Ginger Cookies

- 2/3 cup Wesson Oil (Canola)
- 1 cup sugar

- 1/4 cup molasses (Grandma's)
- 1 beaten egg
- 2 cups sifted enriched flour
- 2 teaspoons soda
- 1/2 teaspoon salt
- 1 teaspoon cinnamon
- 1 Tablespoon ginger
- 1/2 teaspoon nutmeg
- 1 pinch cloves

Cream the shortenings and sugar. Add egg and beat well. Add molasses and mix well. Sift the dry ingredients and add to mixture, stirring until well blended. Cover dough and chill for two hours. Roll into small balls and roll in sugar. Place 2 inches apart on heavy cookie sheet. Bake in oven (350 degrees) for twelve minutes. Makes 48 cookies.

Hot Cross Buns

Use the basic recipe for Sourdough Bread.

Add 1 to 2 extra Tablespoons of sugar, and the following:

- 1 teaspoon cinnamon
- 1/2 teaspoon nutmeg
- 1/2 cup currants or raisins
- 1/2 cup candied orange or any candied fruit, finely chopped

Divide into 30 pieces and shape into balls. Place buns on a lightly greased baking sheet spaced about 1 inch apart. Using floured scissors, snip a cross over the top of each bun, about 1/2 inch deep. Bake at 375 degrees for 12 to 15 minutes. Cool on wire racks. Drizzle icing over the top of each bun, following the lines of the cross.

Icing: Combine

- 1 cup confectioners' sugar
- 4 teaspoons milk or cream
- a dash of salt,
- 1/4 teaspoon vanilla extract.

About the Type

This book utilizes the Bauer Bodoni typeface. It is named after Giambattista Bodoni, a master engraver of the eighteenth and early nineteenth centuries. Established in 1926, this version produced increased legibility, resulting in a graceful and elegant effect.

About the Author

Timothy Roach is a retired marketing vice president of a Boston-based wealth management company. He lives in the Boston area.

Printed in the United States
by Baker & Taylor Publisher Services